Healing The Nations

Rainbow Sun Michelle
Healing the Nations

Copyright © 2025 by Rainbow Sun Michelle

ISBN 979-8-89383-883-1

Healing The Nations

HELPING MEN AND WOMEN HEAL FROM THE
CONSEQUENCES OF HELL THROUGH CHILDLIKE FAITH
PRAYERS THAT ROUT PRIDE AND ARROGANCE

GOD THE FATHER'S ARMOR BEARER

RAINBOW SUN MICHELLE

Contents

Dedication

I dedicate this book to Christ Jesus, my bridegroom, to give divine honor to him and keep my promise to him that more leaders and prophets will start putting Christ Jesus' heart first for people at heart than their major platforms, stages, and hidden agendas of the gospel of faith. Christ Jesus taught me childlike faith that I had to learn to put him first and make what he teaches me priority and first, who died for my sins over 2,000 years ago, and who taught me how to have a saving relationship with him through the eyes of small children at my mom's daycare. I thank Christ Jesus for teaching me the childlike faith, making me a humble pulp because of the importance of having a relationship with him first and walking away from people who did not want me to be Christ Jesus' bride. I did not think I deserved to be loved. Lord Jesus thank you for these prayers for they are my promises to you in which I have lived them in serving you and loved to do so people can learn your heart Christ Jesus and Godly humility and not just your hand, that they will learn to live from the place of your heart and make that their altar of christ jesus heart. Lord Jesus, if I could worship you 1,000 times a month it is my Godly humility and honor to honor you on that type of level. It's a blessing many times to serve you and other days it does not even seem if I'm blessed, but through your atonement over 2,000 years ago I am blessed from that place and believe in the righteousness of your blood, that I drink from you -john 6:54. It's an honor to do your ways and you change my heart about your ways. You teach me lord Jesus to practice what challenges me, you teach me Godly love, though I am still growing in loving people and loving myself, it's still an honor to honor the one who laid down his life for me, and from that place of your heart I live it's just what I love to do. John Bevere said in his book Bait of satan preachers are not what they preach about but what they live. Thank you lord Jesus for teaching me that we should be saving lost souls like it's the last day to live, you taught me street ministry for 5 years, how to save lost souls without bank loans, without a major platform, without a title, and without a high position in the churches, and without fame and popularity being my desire. I just did street ministry because you love me lord Jesus and we together moved from that place out on the streets because we reached out to the undesirables of society because they do not want to step in anyone's churches. Lord Jesus you taught me that is not money I need to start ministry but if I use having a relationship with you and wisdom then I do not have to worry about a major platform to win lost souls closer to you but just Godly wisdom, faith and love for people and your presence lord Jesus. Being a blessing to those around me. Because having a relationship with you lord Jesus is the Godly view of seeing you through the eyes of a child and doing relationship from that place that is the humility pulp you have made me this day and all the divine divine honor lord Jesus is placed on your crossover 2,000 years ago you died for my sins. I live from a place of your cross having childlike faith, where faith begins and failure ends. Not any works people could do, or I could do it is only by your cross lord Jesus. Jesus has given from a place of love and sacrifice thus we do those same things but through the eyes of small children. Honoring you Christ Jesus for all things you have done from that place of your cross over 2,000 years ago. You are first in my heart and my entire life lord Jesus.

I also dedicate this book to God the father because he sent Christ Jesus my way, thank you God the father for all you have done in my life the divine

Glory and divine honor is yours, I always tell you to go the distance being the God you want to be and to just be God and from that day in the garage when you gave me that song to encourage you and be your strength I knew it would what you just love to do. What I have gone through has been for your divine glory and divine honor, I honor you God the father.

I dedicate this book also to God's Godly generals, Godly prophets and people who are suffering and struggling with inward pride and arrogance. Leaders who do not know how to give up their ministries and their churches. They are living to preach in hidden and direct disobedience because they were about the followers and the major platforms. There are many teachers of the gospel who must be healed from pride and arrogance and start doing relationships with Jesus from a child's eyes.

I dedicate this book to my mother, and my male enemies, male relatives, and people suffering from pride and arrogance concerning their hearts and minds. I dedicate this book to you by putting my faith in Christ Jesus atonement for them so through Christ Jesus' cross over 2,000 years ago Christ Jesus would change them through his redemptive work. I pray God Jesus would change their hearts and minds so many of God's generals and people will not be lost from pride and arrogance and will NOT lose their souls from pride and arrogance because they looked at the followers for their own selfish gain, popularity, titles, and high positions in the temples. many people and leaders must come out of the deceitfulness of riches.- Mark 4:19.

God the father says my generals, leaderships, and prophets many of them be lost from pride and arrogance, those in the churches are lost, until they come out themselves, and they do more than just churches buildings serving, there are many churches lacking creativity because they limit me to just staying the same, I'm doing a new thing Isaiah 43:18, I changed my word from Ecclesiastes where it was said there nothing new under the sun, Isaiah 43:18 I changed my mind and my word with my written word.

I wrote this childlike faith book for all people struggling with pride and arrogance for healing from hell, God Jesus had put it on my heart to do a childlike faith book of nothing but pocket prayers that many people could carry on them for prayer a Godly lifestyle, obey prayer, and stay integral to what they pray about. God Jesus told me there are many prophets and leaders living the ministry and preaching in direct disobedience because Christ Jesus told them to give up their churches. These leaders and pastors have disobeyed him and are without him even though they preach with him. Christ Jesus told me that God's generals and leaders and people needed healing from the consequences of pride and arrogance. The money, followers, titles, popularity and the prideful authority of what comes in these ministries who are depending on major platforms to be their main source of income and the followers who lust after their ministries. There are many generals and prophets who make the major platforms a lustful source instead of a Godly love source, when really they could do ministry for under 50 dollars a month or less. I've learned that the ministry does not always have to start with bank loan money or major platforms. It starts with what you sacrifice from your heart, motivated by Christ Jesus' cross of loving those around you and wisdom. A place of Christ Jesus' cross putting our faith in the love God has for all people. So, you sacrifice from a place that you already have yourself rather than looking for other sources of money to do ministry when from the beginning it was never about the money but having a relationship with Jesus and building off his sacrifice over 2,000 years ago. The bible says in psalm 145:8-9 God is good to all and compassionate to all. Many times lost people on the streets and everywhere people go many people in their hearts are looking for you to come to them. They watch how Christ Jesus had a kingdom relationship with his heavenly father. People who watched him went in his direction, and they came in his direction or Jesus used his locator visionary presence to find people and heal them. Some leaders do ministry from higher places of ministries when really most kingdom work is out of the churches. I've seen many leaders choose major platforms over the presence of the lord. Major platforms are producing the presumptuous sins of pride and arrogance concerning authority. God Jesus told me many generals, leaders, and believers are without him and lost. That should NOT be. We always want to put the relationship with Jesus first instead of leaders making ministry work their addiction of selfish gain because sometimes he could lead you to go to places to bless lost souls than in the churches. I learned in street ministry that many lost souls are street walking and need to experience Jesus' love right where they are in their hearts. Something I have personally lived myself and will continue to live if Christ Jesus lets me. Personally, and honestly saying this, if I rainbow did street ministry with Christ Jesus without a bodyguard then God's generals and leadership have no excuse at all why they are NOT on the streets winning lost souls who do not want to go to anyone's churches because of judgmental leaders. Those generals and leaderships should be praying the blood of Christ Jesus over lost souls and bringing them in from that place. Shame on them!. So, This is a book of just prayers that me and God Jesus put together to help eradicate the presumptuous sins of pride and arrogance of authority that is corrupting generals, leaderships, and believers and they are headed for hell. God Jesus let's get the nations healed from the consequences of hell before they lose their souls from big churches, major platforms of prideful popularity of authority that people flock to churches but take upon themselves the behavior of their leaders and pastors. There are leaders and pastors reeking with that nasty stench of sinful pride and arrogance and on their way to hell, unless they repent and learn how to put down dark addictions of pride and arrogance that are coming from their ministries, major platforms and churches popularity. This book of prayers is for generals, leaders, and believers to get people into a relationship with God Jesus from a place of a small child's eyes. In this book are just Godly honesty and Godly humility prayers that people can move in action to and start saving lost souls like its people's last day to live. What about their relatives, loved ones, and people they do not know, and those who they do know who are friends or friends of the family. They need people who will pray for them and intercede for them. So, these are all Godly child-like faith prayers. I have lived and practiced daily that Christ Jesus taught me to live and make sure I live them before the lord Christ Jesus when I did street ministry for 5 years straight in 2019-2025. I don't quite know how many lost souls got saved but I give Christ Jesus the glory for every love greeting card released out of my hands. God Jesus and I saved close to 50 lost souls a month or 100 lost souls, or 40 lost souls or 30 lost souls a month just God Jesus and me. God Jesus saved my mother, redeemed her soul and healed her from her destruction when a leader in the spiritual realm did not want my mom to have life and cursed me and my mother that our lives be taken away from us. I gave my mother the highest highest honor with my knowledge of God's written word and stepped in for my mother used the word of God for mom to give her soul back and life just like the lord promised my mother. And I honor my mother. My love for my mother is unconditional but not perfectly as I've always shown her love. - God Jesus told me he is not the type of God who is afraid to hang around lost people, they are generals, leaders, and believers who are loved but lost. If only they sacrifice their ways in ministry, they would not be afraid to lose, to gain something that they do not have, that they thought they did." 1 john 2:16

Prayer from God the Father. I do not want my people to love me from a place of pride and arrogance but to love me from the redemptive work of Christ Jesus atonement, who believes in losing to gain the eternal life that my people pray for. It's time for people to be healed from pride and arrogance and I would no longer distant myself from a wayward and stiff necked people who dishonor me, in the way I've taught them to love, I see very few people who read their bibles but yet they do not ask me for the kingdom of heaven, I will give my people the kingdom of heaven when they will be trusted with it, and they have been tried.

There must no longer be the form of godliness of prayer; there must be action done with prayer, not just the profession of prayer. -Matthew 7:21-23.

So, it's the lord's heart. We daily bow our hearts and minds at Christ Jesus' feet to honor the lord and serve him with right hearts and right minds. And having people's best interest at heart, uprightly in heart for them and thinking love thoughts about people. A fresh honor to the Lord Jesus, the wisdom and prayer for God's people to practice what challenges them, but through the action of obeying prayer not just saying prayer. God will fulfill his promises, if we just let him change our hearts and minds. Uprightly daily repenting, and upright daily depending on God's strength so our hearts and minds can be free to serve the lord.

-Amen God Jesus

The nations need healing from hell, but they must humble themselves and choose this day whom they will serve if they want healing from hell. Where would my people be without my mercy? Thus, I god the father hath authority in the universe, and I have sent my rainbow and have bent my bow to offer another dimension of healing for those who want to be saved from hell.

CHAPTER 1

Child~like faith upright Living

CHILD-LIKE FAITH PRAYERS THAT ROUT OUT PRIDE
AND ARROGANCE.

Healing for the nations
Healing the nations from the consequences of hell
through the 8-fold
Written Glory of God
The 8-fold cord written glory of an outpouring of
healing for the nations and God's prophetic mind
changes a fresh Grace and fresh Glory.

The 8-fold cord of the written Glory of God
prophetically changing his mind
It is written, God changed his mind -Psalm 86:13
For great is thy mercy toward all his people and thou
have delivered
Our souls from the lowest hell.

- Matthew 18:3-4 it is written Jesus changed his Mind

Let the lord do this for all his people. It is written

psalm 86:13 over and Over and over repeatedly over again and again.
Healing the nations from the consequences of hell
Because of pride and arrogance

It is written God changed his mind- Jeremiah 18:8

If the nations against which I have spoken turn from its evil. I will relent and reverse my decision concerning the devastation that I intended to do. God the father will have a change of mind and heal us all from hell, he will change his mind and no longer afflict the nations in great judgements. If we change and obey God Jesus
It is written God changed his mind – Ezekial 21:27

I will overturn, overturn, overturn, and it shall be no more, until he comes whose right it is, and I'll give to him. God overturned his judgement again; he changed his mind just because of his people.

It is written that God changed his mind again- Exodus 32:14.

And the lord repented of the evil which he thought to do his people.

God changed his mind and his word again from Ecclesiastics 1:9 said
There is nothing new under the sun
Isaiah 43:18 in the bible I'm doing a new thing

Christ Jesus had a change of mind- mark 2:18-22 it is written Jesus changes everything, for all things are possible with Jesus Matthew 19:26 it is written God's people do not have to remain the same or who they are with
With Jesus, the people of God stay with Jesus.
It is written Isaiah 25:8 god changed his mind he will daily take away hell and death and wipe all our tears away, I'm looking for a people of faith who believe in a new thing, and the repeated 8 fold glory of the written change of mind and word of god of those who need saving power, and who will use these bible verses over and over and over again
Praise the lord right where you are
-Let's go the distance with the lord and let him be the God he wanna be
And to let him Just be God
God the father's prophetic changing wills, prophetic big changes
God's written prophetic changes of mind
-Psalm 57:2 It is written that God performs all things. God has the authority to have a daily change of mind in all things.
Jeremiah 15:19 It is written- God changed his mind. This written word says in Jeremiah 15:19 from God says take back those words and I will take back my words, then my people will stand tall before me, use words truly and well.
It is written Nahum 1:9-12 god changed his mind he will no longer
Afflict his people where he did
Colossians 1:20 It is written and through Christ Jesus

to reconcile To himself all things whether on earth or in heaven, making peace by his blood on the cross.
The 8-fold glory of God of changing his mind found in his written word.
And destroying the curse of hell from off his people's souls because of
Pride and arrogance that God would give his people this Glory.
if they only served him with the right hearts and perfected minds. God the father and the rainbow saving people's souls God cursed to hell, with both our humility and love for people and mercy.
Lord heal this nation, America, from the consequences of hell.
lord heal us all, sin has corrupted this country America and America must repent and have sincere change in the minds and hearts, where so many of God's people and leaders are sinning, when the mind and heart needs a work of healing and not just profession of repentance but true childlike faith change
The healing from hell that comes with walking in love, and putting away sin the gift of change, the gift of love that so many people need, and the healing of repenting that comes with sincere change, that's the healing we need sincere change in our lifestyles, hearts, bodies, and minds God's people need healing from hell.
I feel like God jesus is saying to those who by this book the curses are lifting

Someone said that "the 8- fold glory of God changing his mind cannot be broken.

Isaiah 30:26 says the light of the sun will be seven times brighter, like the light of seven days on the day the lord binds up the brokenness of all his people and heals the wounds he has inflicted. This bible verse is confirmation to my identity as the sun that God will have a change of mind for all his people, he will heal his people where he hurt them. He will heal the nations from hell because he has had a change of mind concerning the nations, the prayers of the sun, use this 8 fold glory each and every day over and over and over again until you get the healing from hell that god's people desperately needed because of the consequences of pride and arrogance.

-May God the father use the 8 fold written glory bible verses over and over and over again and again and over and over again just to save souls For his glory and honor and praise, these are just because prayers and offerings lifted to the Lord for all his people.

God the father says so my people I do not want you to take the false prophetic of leadership in my kingdoms as something that cannot be changed. Jesus my son said thou shalt not tempt the lord thy god and he only shalt the enemy of his wilderness was to serve when he was fasting 40 days and nights. I God the father am always changing my mind, and revoking, and shifting, it's what I have the authority to do. So do not limit me to just be the same, study your bibles and know me for yourself than your leaders and teachers who do not study their bibles and don't teach their congregations how to study the written word. Someone said "this false prophetic is only real for people who put their faith In it", I'm healing my people from hell through Christ Jesus and Rainbow sun, but who will believe and put me first. Who will believe to put me first? Who of my people in my kingdom will live the gospel. My leadership knows that I move according to the seasons, and there is going to be a billion lost soul harvest that revival breaks out in this country America to heal America from hell, healing the nations from the consequences of hell. I'm calling for people who want to live the gospel and not put their faith in what their enemies say and can't see what they say. My people ask me to tweak your vision......seeing sin we sin not hearing sin we think not. -Luke 4:1-12, Matthew 4:1-12

The bible says that many false prophets will go into the world and have not people's best interest at heart- 1 John 4:1. God will protect his people from false prophets; he will change everything for them. - Mark 2:18-22. Jesus changing prophetic wills sin is undone in the lord's name, Jesus will bring prophetic changes to people's lives. because Jesus changes everything, Jesus will change cities, heal nations, change communities, change homes, change families, change people's finances, Jesus will change lost minds and lost hearts, Jesus changes lost souls, Jesus can change sinners, Jesus changes false prophecies, can change people's decisions, and Christ Jesus can change economies. He can change his mind at his authority to do good- mark 2: 18-22 says Jesus changes everything. Christ Jesus a historical changer of everything for his glory and honor. Jesus will take what's evil and make it good for God's people. Jesus will cause the lord to work all things out for his people. Jesus will change prophecies and everything for the written glory of God. God Jesus and God the father this is for your glory and honor and keeping my promises to you. fulfilling the promise made to Christ Jesus in the rose Garden to honor his heart. God is healing his people from hell through childlike faith prayers because someone is praying for them. For people To use this 8 fold glory of written mind changes from the lord over and over and over to the people who believe and want to buy this book, to have the pocket 8 fold prophetic Glory of God written word of changing his mind. I'm talking about the 8-fold glory of God, the father ignoring people's enemies' authority just to love on many people. I'm talking about God the father going the distance to those who will believe and not only believe but obey their prayers and stay integral to their prayers

CHAPTER 2

Child-like faith prayers

ROUTING OUT PRIDE AND ARROGANCE HEALING
THE NATIONS FROM THE CONSEQUENCES OF HELL

–Matthew 18:1-4 says in the bible and Christ Jesus called a little child to him and said to his disciples that unless you humble yourselves as a child you will NOT go to heaven, but those who humble themselves like a child are the greatest in the kingdom of heaven.

-God the father says even my great patriarch of the faith Paul was martyred he was killed for his faith he reaped what he sowed at the end of his life, Paul a former murderer went through many beatings, tribulations, and much persecution, so why should men live in Paul's past, and not think that they will die for the faith like Paul. Paul in the bible was killed under grace, fulfilling every word of his faith.

- NO murderers hath Eternal life because it's not childlike, unless people's repentance comes with change. -Matthew 18:1-3
- NO adultery has eternal life because it's not childlike, unless people's repentance comes with change- Matthew 18:1-3

- NO forms of deception have eternal life; it's not childlike. Unless deception is undone and no longer concealed -Matthew 18:1-4
- NO forms of abuse hath eternal life it's not childlike, unless people change in repentance -Matthew 18:3, Do people humble themselves like a child?
- NO type of judgmental leadership goes to heaven if they do not Walk in love, unless leaders and believers repent, change, and love unselfishly. God the Father and God Jesus do not give people a selfish love, always unconditional, always willing to restore unbiasedly. God is never selfish when it comes to love like a small child always willing to give despite what we have said or done to him. Like small children love when they are wronged by fellow children they get back to interacting like the offense never happened that's how easily they forgive and how easily they are willing to let go of offense in order to continue to love those around them, small children always love people around them, if they know people well or not. You don't have to know people in order to bless them, no, bless people around you despite knowing them or not because it's not always about what you give, it's giving like a child's heart expecting nothing in return. But that recognition will come between you and only the lord. It's what you do In Front of him that matters to him. The recognition is not for you all honor is placed on Christ Jesus and people not being in themselves from their hearts. If people show their ministries to be only in themselves then is it really

God Jesus ministry or is it works of the sinful flesh.-
Matthew 18:3-4

CHAPTER 3

Word from God the father he says:

As I've watched my generals, leaders, and my people do ministry selfishly, they expect their congregations to stabilize their pockets, but they do not heal people the way Jesus did in ministry, this selfish love has displeased me, why is it says the lord that my generals enrichment themselves, they do not have healing ministries, my people lack their heavenly identities and heavenly names, and my churches do not have dream ministries. Churches that are not my churches, how could my generals, leaderships, and my people love so selfishly even after being taught by my spirit on how to walk in love. This has displeased me. My generals, leaderships, and believers need healing from this of loving their congregations selfishly instead of pouring pride and arrogance in my people with their preachings, repent and change, says the lord. Let me take away your big churches, major platforms, and prideful presumptuous authority with titles, and let me give you the kingdom of heaven. Because what I'm seeing from my generals and leaderships, they are without me, though they preach the gospel. They don't show the world my kingdom of heaven, they show themselves. How could my generals, and leadership keep sinning against my heart, but I know, I know they are lost, this is not my perfect will. Give up those things that are a hindrance to eternal life, and I'll give them the kingdom of heaven if they are not afraid to lose what the world gave them to gain me! -Matthew 19:16-30, mark 10:17-31, Luke 18:18-30

CHAPTER 4

Healing prayers from pride and arrogance.

HEALING THE NATIONS FROM HELL

–Lord, I pray that your generals and leadership choices do not let their enrichment from their congregations hinder them from eternal life. deceitfulness of riches. -Mark 4:19

-Lord I'll give up everything just to have you as the young rich ruler did not.-luke 18:18-30.

-Lord i pray let me share my wealth with others around me

-Lord I pray I am wealthy, and I own much but yet your word says the rich lack the kingdom of heaven lord am I willing to give it up to follow you as the young rich ruler was born and could not give up his riches.?-luke 18:18-30

-Lord let what I lose for you, you restore me from another place like the rich young ruler did not see in Luke 18:18-30, what are leaderships and believers attached to that hinders them from eternal life.

-Lord tell me that my riches mean nothing to you, if I don't have you Jesus

-Lord your generals, leaderships, and people may be rich, but their riches could make them be lost.-Mark 10: 17-31

-Lord, let your generals and leaderships give up habitual addictions from sins of enrichment from their congregations. -Luke 18:18-30

-Lord I'm young and rich, but my riches you do not want me to put them first. I will learn from the rich young ruler in the book of Matthew 19:16-30 in the gospel of Christ Jesus who lost eternal life.

-Lord you want to see mega churches, mass ministries, churches buildings pulverized at your feet of mercy and love, where the habitual dark addictions of ministry enrichment, fame, self-honor, titles, high positions, major platforms, or what people and leaderships are attached to are given up to follow jesus.

-Lord, if preachers tell you and people they don't preach for money, then tell them don't ask for it and Lord they are willing to give up their mega churches, mass ministries and churches buildings and titles. -Matthew 18:3 in the bible unless they humble themselves like a child they will not enter into the kingdom of heaven.

-Lord let your generals and leaders do ministry and have a saving relationship with you just like a child would do unto you a child would put you first lord.

-Lord, let not the trap of ministry enrichment be what your generals and leaderships depend on for a self-honor with the world.

-Lord let their be all things possible with you.-Matthew 19:26

-Lord, I pray that things change for me daily as I stay with Jesus.

-Lord, I pray that Jesus has an eternal daily change of mind for all things to work out for my good. Romans 8:28-mark 2:18-22 Everything eternally can be changed with Jesus.

-Lord, I pray that you heal all the nations from hell as they turn to Christ Jesus, because we cannot put the things of this world first before our relationship with him. The lord comes first than any selfish desires or selfish gain in ministry. Matthew 18:1-4

The lord says:
I will dishonor every prophecy that does not come with my love so keep me first. -Corinthians 13:1

The lord says
Their faith based books don't come with love, you writers of lies (Jeremiah 8:8), you false prophets that prophesy to my people and yet I know you not to have people's best interest at heart, the titles of your faith based books may sound good to most, but if your books are very judgmental and very critical of many others than why should I draw people to read your books if it's not who it says it really is by the title of your books.

The Lord says
I'm willing to save my people if your repentance is not based on your flesh to not have faith in my ways of having a relationship with me or your ministries.
-Lord, let leaders and generals honor individuals in their congregations, let them call up all the poor people up to their altar for financial blessing from their own bank accounts so their congregations don't leave poor and sick like they came in their churches. Matthew 18:3-4

The Lord says
Many of my generals and leaders leave their congregations sick and poor

they don't heal like jesus did, and they are more focused on what they wanna preach my leaders hath lied in their giving to my people, left them sick and weeping for healing, but yet my people are suffering from lack of healing in their churches, and my leaderships hath left my people sick, without interpretation for their dreams, and impoverished in their churches. This needs to stop in churches that are not my churches.

-Lord, I pray that the leaders honor God Jesus' heart for his glory first. To always put honoring the lord's heart without recognition on tv, or social media, nor recognition from their congregations. All honor is placed on Christ Jesus' heart. Matthew 18:1-4

-Lord, I pray that the leaders honor your heart first, let them drink from the glory of your heart's desires and please you from that place of having a relationship with you.

-Lord, I pray that leaders and believers don't cover up their true motives in ministry. Lord, let your leadership do relationships and ministry from a place of your heart. Lord let not leaderships misuse people in their congregations to cover up their personal motives, but to love the people in their congregations and not let them leave the same way they came. Matthew 18:1-4

-Lord let not leaderships despitefully misuse their congregations for self- enrichment, leaderships must not continue to preach in places of unfulfillment because of knowledge. Ministries must put away the nuptial bed and go back to the lost sheep and forsake the 99.-psalm 139, matthew 18

-Lord, I pray to God the Father to ask your generals and leadership if they are willing to give up their big churches for eternal life. -Matthew 18:1-4

-Lord, let leaders in churches heal your people from cancer the way Jesus did, let them not preach what their head knowledge wants to preach and not overlook the sick who are around them. Ministries and Leaderships should not forsake the sick in their ministries just to preach head knowledge.-Matthew 18:1-4

-Lord let not leaders and generals forsake the sick in their churches ministries to get recognized by the rich.

-Lord, I pray that I do not forsake my enemies to get recognized by the rich. -lord, let me Love my enemies and do something sweet and kind for them despite their hearts or sins because the heavenly father would want that in his heart. -Matthew 5:43-44

-Lord, I pray that leaders and generals honor their enemies, do good to them if they have the power to, and celebrate the lives of their enemies without asking for anything in return. -Matthew 18:1-4

-Lord let your generals call up their enemies they know of and see how they are doing, give your enemies food if they are hungry, clothe them if they are lost, and restore them if they are willing to change their lives. -Matthew 18:1-4

-Lord, I pray that people celebrate the lives of others they don't know, on their jobs, in the streets, and in the stores and homes. celebrate your enemies, and love them like a child expecting nothing in return. -Matthew 18:1-4

-Lord, I pray that your leaders and generals answer their servants' cries, call their servants personally and ask them how their day is going at work, see how their families are doing, and see how their lives are changing in your ministry. and see where their hearts are, if they need any counseling, or just your love. It's not how big the church is, it's about those who serve their leaders and teachers. -Matthew 18:1-4

-Lord let leaders be delivered from church buildings, or how about leaders personally call up every servant to see if they need personal time with you, or maybe they might need money, or they might need help with their lives. see how they are doing personally and not just their serving in ministres as orphans. -Matthew 18:1-4

-Lord, I pray that leaders come to you as a child giving all of themselves to you. -Matthew 18:1-4

-Lord, let not your leaders or generals seek their own honor to forsake the sick in their ministries. they must love those around them. -Matthew 18:1-4

-Lord, let not your leaders and generals forsake their servants needs to get recognized by rich people, let not leaders and generals forsake the rich and poor in their ministries to serve God, or be around other rich people in the ministry. -Matthew 18:1-4

-Lord let not leaders forsake their servants to serve God in ministry, get to know your servants on a daily basis. Matthew 18:1-4

-Lord let leaders and generals have honor to Christ Jesus childlike, engage in the lives of their servants if they got big churches, throw it at Christ Jesus feet and put away get more intuned with people on the streets, and in homes. -Matthew 18:1-4

-Lord let your leaders and generals honor their servants like a child would celebrate people just because. -Matthew 18:1-4

-Lord let your leaders and generals take care of their enemies like they do their servants, -Matthew 18:3.

-Lord, I pray let your leaders and generals not forsake prayer to those on the streets, let them humble themselves as a child and work with their servants, pay them for talents, don't condemn those who serve you, ad most of all servants should not be the only ones doing their teachers work. -Matthew 18:1-4

Lord Jesus you just spoke:
-I need to use you when I call you to me for my Glory.
Matthew 18:1-4

-Lord, I pray that more leaders and generals would use their authority in a childlike faith lifestyle to sacrifice for the needs and prayers of their servants and congregations, and have the type of spirit that will lay down your life for your servants and God's people. -Matthew 18:1-4

-Lord, I pray that your generals and leaders do NOT take the credit for the ministry work their servants only did.- Matthew 18:1-4

-Lord, let your generals and leaders honor their enemies like a child. -Matthew 18:1-4

-Lord, I pray I do not forsake the poor people around me to get recognized by the rich, our enemies lives come first before selfish gain in ministries. -Matthew 5:43-44

-Lord, I pray that leaders and generals forsake their enemies to get recognized by the rich, and honor their enemies with their lives. What reward do they have if they only love the ones who love them? Matthew 5:43-44.

-Lord let your leaders and generals call their lost family members daily, let not their forsake families to get recognized by the rich people, but serve their family members how they serve God. -Matthew 18:1-4

- Lord, I pray that I give my enemies God's best interest at heart. God the father will honor your prayers for them, it's about love and humility covering people. Bringing changes in their lives. Matthew 18:1-4

-If you know lost people in your families, visit them, pray for them if they be in your spirit from the lord, do not forsake the lost in your families to get recognized by the rich, lost people come first in ministries than a Sunday paycheck from congregations for materialistic things and self-enrichment. Matthew 18:1-4

-pray for people who the world looks down on because they follow Christ Jesus, if you see them struggle in the spirit realm, do something really sweet for them.-matthew 18:1-4

-never give false judgements to those who are repenting, especially if they are putting away sin and are obeying the lord.-matthew 18:1-4

-Lord let not the pharisee spirit in God's kingdoms call something good evil, let them ask of something they want to humble themselves the pharisees could have had what Christ Jesus had on him if they only asked the pharisees went to hell over 2,000 years ago just because they had habits of not asking for what they wanted with jealousy in their hearts. Matthew 18:3

-Lord let leaders celebrate their congregations daily who give their churches money, celebrate your congregations who pour in their pockets.-Matthew 18:1-4

-Restore your enemies if they repent with change, never forsake their healing and need to get recognized by the rich people.- Matthew 18:1-3

-If you see your enemies struggling in the spirit realm do not condemn them for what they say, look at their hearts before you speak against them. God could want to make them your friends but people look at their actions, don't always judge people by their actions, their hearts God has his eyes on. - Matthew 18:1-4

-Lord let leaders align their hearts with the title names of their churches.

-Lord you have rejected hell because mercy said no, it's really sweet of the lord to do this for all his people the journey he wants to take with his people, healing the nations from the consequences of hell, the lord in this book has rejected hell, he's bringing new dimensions of healing, greater healing for all his people. The lord the judge is rejecting hell. Give the lord a yes lord, stop what you're doing and thank god for being so so so so good to his people, and never failing love, thank the lord celebrate him every day, win lost souls like he is winning yours, do unto others how you want the lord to do unto you. **the lord got someone praying for his people because breaking news the lord the judge has rejected hell.**

The lord says:
-Leaderships let me align your hearts with your churches greeting titles names, that people see, why should the churches names draw people to come in, when many churches are a den of thieves and wolves, and God said his house shall be called a house of prayer. Repent the lord The judge has rejected hell.

CHAPTER 5
More childlike faith prayers

lessing people who saluted my name, serving those who
have hurt me in this book, humbling myself like a
child, washing people's hearts and minds, saving souls
with love, love, love, love and love.- Matthew 18:1-4

-Do not forsake your own family to get recognized by the
rich, love your people and family, visit them and pray for them.
humble yourselves like a child. Choose love, choose the lord,
and choose to keep him first.- Matthew 18:1-4

-When was the last time leaders called their lost relatives
and prayed with them, how can the richest leaders be the
poorest people if they don't have love in their hearts for people
around them. -Matthew 18:1-4

-God has the authority to put people in places where only
the word of God will bring them out. God has authority over
people who don't like you, but his word is for you, what reward
do people or leaderships have if they only pour into people
who like them. -Matthew 18:1-4

-A Rich leadership will serve the poor in their congregations, the poor may not always have money to give in their

ministries, but God will crown the poor in ministries with a throne of honor. -1 Samuel 2:8

-The bible says the rich people are the footstool of the poor, when will rich leaders celebrate poor people in their ministries. Matthew 18:1-4.

-Lord let leaders see that when Christ Jesus preached in the temples, he healed the sick his way around him, instead of preaching from his own. Christ Jesus preached in the temples, but it was not preaching of his own. He took time preaching the knowledge of love to love people around him. Poured healing in their lives, gave to them from the kingdom of heaven. Matthew 18:1-4

The Lord says

If churches are too big that leaders and generals can tend to their servants personally or intimately as saying private professional healing or counseling then put away your buildings? What are hearts really for in ministry? What do leaders and minds and hearts call ministry? God knows hearts so people should not have ministry anxiety, sometimes what comes with ministry is the sin that god wants to save people from. -Matthew 18:1-4

-Lord if your generals and leaderships are finding women on the streets to sleep with and they are already married men, then let them be accountable for using their visionary skills to not find lost souls or homeless people on the streets and bring them into their churches to Give them jobs in their businesses and churches, give them a home, and provide for impoverished people from their congregation earnings. -Matthew 18:1-4.

-Lord, let me honor you with my first fruits. -Proverbs 3:10-11

-Lord, let me honor you with my eyes, body, mind, lifestyle

and heart just like a child would humble themselves. -Matthew 18:1-4.

-Lord, I pray let leaderships and people honor you first before any selfish desires of their own.- Matthew 18:3-4

-Lord let honoring you as first exceed men's self- honor. Matthew 18:3-4

-Lord let leaders and people honor those on the streets by pointing them to Christ Jesus' cross over 2,000 years ago and that he died for them. -John 3:16

-Lord, I pray let not your son's lust to commit adultery with other men's wives and they are already married to wives of their own home, what type of example do they set for their children who watch them, your Sons bringing curses on their churches, and in their families for adultery. -Matthew 18:3

-Lord, I pray if I see homeless and impoverished people living on the streets in my new car I will do something about it. I will bring change in their lives because God's prophets should be servants of bringing change and praying for people. If leaders have a business of their own maybe they can hire homeless people in their business, give to them and feed them, Iet them give to them from a place they already have that you gave them lord. Lord let not leaders serve you from a place of self-enrichment but always humbling themselves like a child. - Matthew 18:1-4.

-Lord let not your leaderships and generals use kingdom authority for adultery and rebellion, but to repent and humble themselves like a child using their authority to love and do good to people, and not for selfish gain, pride exists when kingdom authority is being used for the good of all, not their pockets. - Matthew 18:1-4

-Lord, let leaderships, people, and generals see their brothers and sisters in prisons, psych wards, drug rehabs, hospitals, street walkers and homeless shelters and put on clothes like them to visit them and meet them right where they are in their hearts to bless people with God's love -Matthew 25:35-46 - Matthew 18:1-4.

-Lord, I pray let your leaderships and generals understand a matter and act upon their understanding they should humble themselves like a child and ask the lord how can they obey him in the areas of surrendering their big churches, surrender what's in their pockets to people who need of them around them and they do what the lord puts on their hearts to do for people around them in their congregations or out at places.- Matthew 18:1-4

-Christ Jesus would act upon his understanding, and not just know like the Pharisees. False witnesses shall not go unpunished. -proverbs 19:9

-Lord maybe leaderships and people can wake up in the morning asking the lord how he's doing, what's on the lord's hearts for him this day to obey him and how can they serve and please him this new day? Lord don't let people leave their houses in the morning without speaking to you before they go out because of these end times. Matthew 18;1-4

-Lord let me honor you every day you wake me up how can i be a blessing and honor people in my day today with you, because i want my relationship with you to be more than just a church building, or high position of popularity and fame i'll humble myself greater than a child to worship you, and throw myself at the feet of your cross. Lord, I honor you. Matthew 18:1-4

-Lord, I'll honor you by giving all of myself to you as first in my heart. -Matthew 18:1-4.

-Lord, I pray that I sacrifice my own authority in ministry to put the needs of those around me first in Christ Jesus' way. - Matthew 18:1-4

-Lord let people and leaders celebrate you in their journey

with you everyday, our day should start off lord how can I please you this day? Anything on your heart I should do? lord jesus how can i humble myself like a child and celebrate you, i'll celebrate you my difficult times and good times but to celebrate you is an honor i will commit to. -Matthew 18:1-4

-Lord, let not generals and leaderships put themselves over your authority, let them humble themselves like a child and obey the lord between only them and him. Childlike faith obedience to the lord must be privately and not only publicly. Matthew 18:1-4

-Lord, let me serve you only between me and you, because it's not about me getting recognized by other people in ministry or my relationship with you, it's for your Glory. Matthew 18:1-4.

-Lord, I pray if leaders, generals and believers have people lost in their families, let them not just watch their loved ones struggle in the spirit realm, that's pride and arrogance of the eyes, lord let families humble themselves like a child and do blessings for their lost loved ones. Let families labor for lost loved ones to see them saved and redeemed. matthew 18:1-4

-Lord, I love the way you teach me to humble myself. I am teachable like a child, lord I humble myself to honor you in public as well as my private time with you. Matthew 18:1-4

The lord says;
I am calling my men to change their mind from crooked mindsets. for crooked mindsets no good thing with the lord. -Proverbs 17:20

-Lord let not generals, leaderships, and believers forsake their family to get recognized by the rich because of false gain in their hearts. When was the last time they called their lost relatives, when was the last time they called the poor and impoverished and took up offerings for them in their congregations. Lord, I pray to heal your generals and leaderships from hell lord when are your generals, prophets, teachers and believers going to stop self enrichment, because self enrichment was never what jesus did in ministry he actually located people to love on them, he located people to save lives, and he located people because he was never doing ministry from ways of his own but by the spirit.

-God the father says my word says: 2 timothy 3:2 men will be lovers of themselves, pride and arrogance is sending many leaders and generals to hell, but I will heal them all from hell, i'll send my word and heal them from destruction for their healing. -psalm 107:20, i'll take away their mega churches, mass ministries, and churches buildings because of the pride of life and their ministries not being marked for heaven, I'll save them from pride and arrogance and give them the kingdom of heaven for the mark of salvation, than the mark of the devil on their churches names, when people drive by their ministries. -Matthew 4:1-12, Luke 4:1-12.

-Lord are churches building titles really who the preachers in those buildings really who they say they are? let's stop deceiving people with good title ministry names, and sermons that have good titles but its not what the sermon really is when preached, sometimes the truth of things are not in ministry titles of sermons or buildings until hearts are exposed.....the name of wicked churches buildings shall rot.-proverbs 10:

-Leaders and generals make your churches identities align up with your hearts and minds, God doesn't need bisexual ministries or adulterous ministries, or warlock satanic ministries, neither condemning ministries, God Jesus cannot use ministries that don't have love from the heart.

The lord says:
In Matthew 4:1-12, Luke 4:1-12 in the bible Christ Jesus turned down the mark of the beast, how much more will mega churches, churches buildings, and mass ministries turn down the mark of the beast for salvation. Healing all the nations from the consequences of hell through childlike faith prayers that rout out pride and arrogance, and save a generation of leaderships who are not marked for salvation in heaven, because the name of their churches their hearts have to align with who they want to draw to their churches, we must not forget that Christ Jesus chose 12 apostles. If my leaderships are not doing ministry for money then pulverize their buildings at my feet, and i'll save their souls from being headed to hell for pride and arrogance, and not showing the world my kingdom of heaven, but only revelations of knowledge and their mouths, did not covid 19 teach them with masks to watch their mouths. I the lord do not want to have another pandemic where people go to hell for their mouths, no breaking news I have rejected hell, repent Mercy said no. People are drawn to those with good hearts, not good churches buildings names. Christ Jesus said if he be lifted up he shall draw all men unto him. – john 12:32

-Lord, I pray that your generals, leaders, and believers get out on the streets and win lost souls closer to Christ Jesus, lord heal them from their choices of their congregation enrichment. Lord, heal all your generals, leaderships, and believers, lord heal them from pride and arrogance in this area. They don't need bodyguards they need love from their hearts Lord, I pray heal them all from hell. Lord ministry does not start with money; people need wisdom, love, and faith around them.

-The greatest wealth that leaders would ever have is NOT found in people's pockets. How many leaders continue to preach in their churches when blind people come in their churches and they leave blind, or cancer people who give their churches most of their money and they leave their churches still with cancer. Never want people to put your ministry first if your heart and mind is at a place of unfulfillment. -psalm 139

Lord let leaders and generals should never be anxious for the ministry when your heart is only for preaching, there has to be some kind of care that leaders put forth to the personal needs of others. -Matthew 18:1-4

God Jesus wants his ministry leaders and generals to not only preach, and not leave people the same around them. Matthew 18:1-4

-Lord i pray for leaders that they not be the cause their staff go to hell, and don't pay their staff but misuse them for their labor, do not take the time to know their staff, leaders who condemn them their staff if they wanna go to other ministries because of how leaders treat their staff. Lord Jesus heal these leaders from the same hell they meant for their staff, and heal their staff from what was spoken over their lives from their leaders. That is not the way leaders do ministry.

-Lord, I pray that your generals, leaders, and believers find people who cannot do for themselves on the streets, and bless people. leaders don't have to know them to bless them, it's just something they should do from their hearts because God has the best interest for all. the lord said in his word that he would that no generals, leaderships, and believers should not perish but all come to repentance. -Peter 3:9

-Lord, I pray that your generals, leaders, and believers honor those who serve under their leadership, instead of leaders receiving the ministry honor only for themselves in front of their congregations and staff when there are people in their ministries helping them. Lord heal your generals from self- enrichment, heal them from greed, and heal them from their churches buildings lord heal them. - Healing for the nations

-Lord, let me forgive because Christ Jesus forgave me, I'll humble myself like a child and forgive people. I'll offer your forgiveness to those who did not like me. Lord, I pray to give me the grace to forgive people. Lord you resist the proud but give Grace to the humble.-James 4:6-7, the first will be last and the last first.-Matthew 20:16

-Lord, I forgive all I can from my heart with your strength to forgive people with your strength even if it's not perfect because Christ Jesus died not perfectly but his heart still loved people, I will still practice forgiveness lord because Christ Jesus forgave me. Lord, let not your generals, leaderships, and believers not be unforgiving servants. -Matthew 18

-Lord, I pray that people do not fast for selfish gain, or selfish desires to be sharper than others in the spirit realm, fasting should be done in love and winning lost souls. Fasting is built on loving others not for selfish ambitions of ministry. Someone said this seen but not heard -Isaiah 58:6-7.

-Lord, I pray to put new thoughts in my mind that please you, mercifully lord Jesus take out bad thoughts and change my mind by staying with you. lord, take sin out the minds of your people, lord heal our minds and heal hearts, don't let our minds send people to places they do not want to be. Lord let all people change the way they think, lord heal people's minds from fear, doubt, and sinfulness. Lord healing for the nations, lord heal them all from hell, lord your abundant in supernatural healing, healing dimensions, washing healings, saturations of healing, lord let supernatural healing detox us, our minds and hearts daily, our inner spirits and inner souls, lord penetrate healings in the nations. Lord cleanse and heal, that we live clean and stay clean. People should not serve you with unholy minds, lord you tell us to choose if we will be clean or not. That's our decision, not his heart to clean people who live and wanna be unclean.. matthew 18:1-4

-Lord I pray thank you for the mind of Christ.

-Lord let our minds be renewed by your holy spirit.

-Lord I pray to break evil thoughts off many many many people's minds, lord put healing in our minds, thinking is a choice, lord break yokes, and break mind control, break cycles, break pride and arrogance off lives. Lord heal all the nations, so you will not be displeased at your people as a whole because of the many nations sinning. Lord, I pray for healing for the nations, if they repent and change.

-Lord, I pray these are the endtimes let us not sin because of the times, lord let the nations heal from sin. lord healing in every place of the nation's lives.

The lord says:

Folks we are in the pre-tribulation God the father is saying my people we have entered into the pre tribulation, I'm doing rapture in the nations for healing, their will be many left behind, and many to a few caught up to meet Christ Jesus, when I do the rapture I'm leaving churches buildings behind, pulverize your churches buildings at my feet, for I only needed 12 people, you trade your ministries for the rapture and I guarantee you those who sacrifice and not afraid to loose, can and will be raptured we are in the pre-tribulation and that's how near we are to the rapture.

The lord says:
Rainbow my armor bearer has a rapture piece, and I brought it to life, when she was watching eagles on the internet, from the floodings of last year the days of Noah, and to biblical prophecy, and I just told rainbow to look at her computer, and she saw the word pre to the bottom of her computer, aligned up with pre tribulation, rapture is so near, but their will be many people left behind, because they believed in falsehood and what's unclean than eternal life.

The lord says:
My people look up in the bible on google where in the bible does it talk about Norway, that's is the exact same place the antichrist is from who will rule the world starting off in trade and targeting governments and world leaders, and these days he's on American soil doing just that, but at the beginning stages.

-Lord, I pray let all people be teachable and obey you because you love us and have our hearts at your best interest, we all humble ourselves like a child ever trusting ever dependent on you, for a greater grace and glory that only comes through Christ Jesus' atonement over 2,000 years ago.

-Lord, let generals, and leaders serve you with new minds and new hearts so they can humble themselves like a child and reach your glory. Lord, let not your generals, leaderships, and believers have minds filled with evil, pride and arrogance. Lord let our minds and hearts be humble, lord we humble ourselves because God hates pride and arrogance, God hates evil, though he loves us through it, he gave us Christ Jesus to repent and be healed from hell.

-Christ Jesus love conquered all things, endured all things, believed all things, and hoped for all things, may people be healed by Christ Jesus unconditional love in these end times, lord Jesus let your love saturate the earth realm, saturate hearts, saturate minds, and saturate lives, lord I pray don't take away your love from the many nations, lord heal them of their sins. Lord heal the nations, lord heal leaders and generals from pride and arrogance.

-Lord, let leaders live humbly before you, you will teach the humble your way. You will guide all the humble in justice - psalm 25:9-14.

-Lord all your paths are mercy and truth, I'm thankful and I humble myself like a child. Christ Jesus' blood covers me over 2,000 years ago, lord you see people through his atonement needing to repent, or daily repent for grace.

-Lord, I pray break all our minds and hearts with your love, lord pour love and goodness on all our minds and hearts so we do not sin mentally neither from our hearts, we will have humble hearts and humble minds that please you, instead of our choices, lord you give us choices, let us all make right choices with Christ Jesus strength and help. matthew 18:1-4

-Lord, I pray that the rapture heals all evil in your peoples lives.

-Lord, I pray that the nations humble themselves and repent and turn to God Jesus, the supernatural healer of evil.

-Lord, I pray saturate the people of God with the supernatural anointings of the rapture, I speak rapture dimensions, creative raptures, creative raptures and rapture healings to activate in this earth realm, in their homes, churches, schools, communities, and businesses.

-Lord, I pray that leaderships, generals, and believers bring changes to lost loved ones in their families headed to hell, lord heal. Lord let leaderships and generals, believers bring changes in their families lives, as prophets are called to bring changes in people's lives, lord redeem, and daily restore, as there is repentance.

The lord says:
When I rapture a people their big churches buildings are left behind things they were attached to like the rich young ruler left behind by Christ Jesus with his riches, and God's people healed and separated from the earth realm through the rapture, it will be rapture miracles for the few who will be caught up in the air.

Rapture will be healing for all the nations, many people healed from every evil, many people healed from sickness, many people healed from diseases, many people healed from destructions, and many healed from sin that's saves people from hell- lord heal all the nations, lord your love endures forever, lord your love is from everlasting to everlasting to those who love you.

The lord says
My people why are you so distracted on rainbow, when the antichrist who will rule the world in trade buying and selling is from Norway, rainbow is just a distraction that worship artist are singing about, when the antichrist is already on American soil, take your eyes off just watching rainbow, these are the end times, and pray for your families and lost relatives than listening to bisexual already married famous gospel worship artist who are lesbians In heart who use music to seduce people in a relationship with them, No MAM they need the holy ghost to live right and want to live right instead of seducing people in the flesh and they are adultery married women, what

will their husbands to do them? What should men do to their wives that cheat on them in their hearts for unclean desires for same sex relationships. Homosexuality should come out of gospel music? What men think about their wives cheating on them, so do they.

God don't give already married women unclean desires for the same sex. That's not how we sing worship music. There are prophets who have stopped listening to this day's gospel music because by hearts it's not holy worship, its from unclean desires that their husbands are not fulfilling in their marriages. So many women are being abused by their husbands because of the lack of faithfulness. Matthew 18:3 in the bible unless they humble themselves like a child in worship they will not enter into the kingdom of heaven.

-Lord your Mercy changes me because I fear you, lord I humble myself as like a child, and give you no lip, but a fresh daily yes lord, I'll take time out my day lord just to give you a fresh yes lord, I'm not too busy with ministry work we're I can't humble myself like a child and thank you..Matthew 18:1-4

-Lord i pray for leaders and believers to not be too busy with their ministry or personal lives that they say can't go to the sick people in their churches and servants lives, lord i pray let them humble themselves and go to the sick people to heal them. Sometimes the ministry is not about people's personal lives, but for other people to proclaim the Glory of God.

-Lord, let your leaders and generals pray for healing over their servants' lives. Matthew 18:1-4

-Lord I pray lord let NOT leaders and generals or believers be too busy in ministry work to humble themselves like a child and go to the lost sheep of the gospel of faith on the streets around them. they don't need a bodyguard just to win lost souls around me. Like my grandmother said for God she lived for God she died. Many people should not be afraid to die for Christ Jesus, so why should leaders and generals base their comfort zones of preaching only around their congregations.

-Lord let leaders in mega churches, mass ministries, and big churches let the leaders of those churches take 2 or 3 people with them and do ministry on the streets, it could be homeless people on the streets other people drive past, that the leaders sent were meant to serve them.

-Lord let the rich serve the poor. -matthew 18:1-4

-Lord let the poor forsake the rich. -matthew 18:1-4

-Lord let those leave the pulpits to have a sincere ministry. -matthew 18:1-4

-lord, I pray to purge sin and evil from all hearts and minds, lord you said in your word that you will give sound hearts and remove any evil or sin, lord I pray sound hearts for all the nations. Lord, I pray to heal hearts and heal minds, healing for the nations. I speak the name of Jesus over every heart and mind, our restless minds need peace, but if we can just relax our thoughts in divine supernatural healing saturations, we will be healed inwardly from sin.

-Lord let me humble myself like a child, and love those around me in my congregation, because having a relationship with you lord is not all about all my preaching sick people in my congregation come first before head knowledge of the bible.

-Lord, I pray let your generals, leaders, and believers put people's healings first, then want their congregation's money in their pockets. Lord, I pray that prayer in churches be attached to any amount of money. Lord pride and arrogance is costing lost souls, lord heal the nations from the consequences of hell this I ask.

-Lord, let not your generals, leaders, and believers' enrichment themselves when people in their ministries are dying from sickness, the sick people, poor people, needy people, impoverished people around them come first in their congregations. Lord, when was the last time your generals and leadership honored their congregations.

-Lord let me honor my enemies on the streets to do something out of love for them without harming them, lord let me honor those in my family who are enemies, don't let me be afraid to favor those who don't like me in their hearts I humble myself like a child. Matthew 18:1-4

-Lord, I learn from Christ Jesus' cross that the highly favored of heaven who was Christ Jesus humbled himself like a child and favored those who did not know anything about him though they saw him face to face. This is humility, the favorable like Christ Jesus humble themselves as a child and show favor to others, even if they don't really love you in their hearts. This is love and this is doing good, did not Christ Jesus favor those who he died for and honored them.

-Like a child you do not have to harm people because they offended you, get back into interacting with people as though the offense never happened. This is childlike faith. Learn how to interact with people despite their offenses. Great peace to those who love God's law and nothing shall offend them.-Psalm 119:165

-Like a child would not look down on people in your hearts, want the best for all people but at heart just like small children interact with children their ages, and they really know nothing about each other. They just keep loving their childhood playmate's despite the offense. matthew 18:1-4

-Lord, let not your generals and leadership forsake their congregations healing around them. They must put their congregations' needs first more than what congregations' money are giving their pockets.

-lord, cause me to keep my covenant with you, I humble myself like a child and stay with Jesus. Matthew 18:1-4

-Lord Jesus you spoke hell over the Pharisees and you humbled yourself like a child to take it away from them if they repented and brought repentance with fruits of change. If you said it you can take it away through repenting and repentance and sincere change.

-Lord, what about people's dreams being interpreted in churches, then just their pastors living their dreams of enrichment, pride and arrogance. What about the churches' money being personally invested in people's dreams in their congregations. -Matthew 18:1-4

-Lord, I pray for the generals and leaders and the servants who serve them. Leaders better humble themselves like a child and invest into their servants personally or their servants will go to other ministries.

-churches ministries without love are only empty buildings.-

-Christ Jesus did teamwork with his disciples, and not people just serving a leadership to live out the dreams of these days's leaders and preachers. They should not love their congregations as servants selfishly only for their ministry work. How could these leaders so selfishly love people who serve them and they misjudge their servants and condemn them. These types of selfish leaderships could lose workers who sow in their leaderships could go to other ministries.

God the father says my generals and leaderships churches are just too big, what happened to personal interaction with their servants. These churches are too big; they don't even know their staff by name, but yet they condemn their workers, and take the credit for what their servants did. Let me teach my generals and leadership how to start ministry for under 50 dollars a month, with no bank loans, no bodyguards. My generals, leadership, and believers could start off ministry under 50 dollars a month and under 1,000 dollars a year. And God Jesus brings in an abundance with the resources you already have and the kingdom of heaven that Christ Jesus had in manifesting healing, it was by his level of sacrifice of love he did unto the holy father that he was able to manifest healing on levels the pharisees were jealous of, because he gave up things in ministry that he did not need. -Matthew 4:1-12

The lord God the father told me he said do not be deceived at ministries you see on tbn, daystar, or the word network, internet popular radio stations, and big mega ministries, or ministries on tv, or internet because most of them serve satan. because their devil murderers, money hungry, devil adulterers, devil false prophets, devil hypocrites, warlocks, satanists, witches, their pockets are fat with self enrichment, and many wolves in sheeps clothing, the lord said do not be deceived my people at this look at their hearts. My people do not be deceived by their popularity, their titles in ministry, position, fame or wealth, nor how many followers they have. Many of them don't heal like Jesus did, they have no homeless people in their homes that they serve or will buy food for, and they dont walk in love. Their crooked minded men and women leaders on these christian tv stations, internet, and mega churches and until they give it up they are lost leaders. Matthew 4:1-12, Luke 4:1-12.

-Lord let not generals and Leaderships not held their congregations back individually from knowing God's promises, that is so selfish for these days leaderships to know the promises of God for their servants who serve them and not tell them because their leaders want the honor in ministry work and recognition, when really, it's their servants who did their work. Believers that's not the type of ministry you want to submit under, no use your discernment about crooked leaderships, and let God Jesus give you biblical knowledge in the word of God what leaderships are speaking over their servants to reverse it and leave those leaderships churches and ministries. God Jesus would not condemn his servants to keep serving him, that's not the way leadership should do ministry. Mathew 18:3

-Lord I'll keep bowing my heart and mind in humility and humbling myself like a child at the cross of Christ Jesus feet if you only give me your son Jesus in a special way that pleases him, lord everything Christ Jesus tells me to do is a yes lord but with my heart and mind. All honor placed upon Christ Jesus cross over 2,000 years ago, never my own honor in my heart.-Matthew 18:3

-Lord let leaders honor their servants for their sacrifices to the ministry. Matthew 18:1-4

-Lord how many leaders know their servants by name in their churches, do they take time out from busy ministry work to personally teach them, leaders should not be so caught up in ministry and not spend personal love time with their servants this is humility and humbling themselves like a child.-Matthew 18:1-4

-Lord, I pray let me humble myself, lord fill my mind and thoughts with humility and love, lord change my mind daily until wicked thoughts are eternally broken off by your daily love lord. Leaders, believers, and generals should not be thinking wickedly at their servants or people and they could make a difference in their lives, and bless those around them. Matthew 18:1-4

-Lord let, rich people, rich preachers and generals give away cars they don't drive, clothes they don't wear, wealth they dont use and materialistic things they lay aside and don't use to people in their congregations or homeless people out in the streets around them, what about the poor, or impoverished around them. How many empty bedrooms do their big houses have, they could locate homeless people out on the streets and bring them into their homes.

-God the father says leaders and generals get around your servants and bless them, labor with their burdens, help them personally with their struggles, personally pray for them, and always know them by name, leaders give your servants what you make off preaching money and income, check to see if their family is okay, if you will personally visit their families, invest in your servants dreams, interpret their dreams and help them with God's promises, just don't let them work your dreams in churches, and not ever deposit love in their lives, that's misusing servants, clean your churches with them, invite them to your mansions, when they wash dishes from churches dinners leaders be washing dishes with them be right there with your servants cleaning those dishes and take concern for their personal needs. minister to your servants while you wash dishes with them When was the last time my generals and leaderships took off their suits and cleaned their own churches, left their mansions to go find homeless people on the streets instead of finding already married women, called the impoverished in their churches and their families in their churches congregations. I will heal these types of ministries and churches from hell if they are willing to humble themselves, and repent.

-Lord, I pray to remove any evil from my mind or sinful way. You did not give me a spirit of evil but of love and power and of a sound mind.- 2 timothy 1:7

-lord, I pray let the nations change the way they think, lord heal all of our thinking and thoughts. Cover all the minds and hearts with Christ Jesus atonement over 2,000 years ago. Lord, intercede for all the nations a divine outpouring of healing of Godly love, Glory love, Godly love, and godly love. Lord Jesus saturate an outpouring of your healing love to heal all the nations of their sins. Lord, I prophesy to you love lord. Go the distance being the god you want to be and just be God.

-Lord let all people be saturated with Godly love until they all melt like wax.

-Lord, I pray to give love dreams, healing dreams, and love visions in the nations. Lord heal with your love, you don't delight in wrath, you love first lord this I pray holy father in Jesus name

-Lord Jesus, I pray pour out your divine healing oil on evil minds and evil hearts there ain't any sinner that you can't save for your glory lord Jesus lord heal the nations.

-Lord Jesus I pray heal evil mindsets, change the lifestyles of our thoughts. - Your love lord conquers evil.

-Lord Jesus, I pray Thoughts of peace, wisdom, faith, love, godly obedience, and godly integrity will be established in the thoughts of all the nations. Lord heal our thoughts. - Jesus' love conquers all evil.

-Lord just let your love conquer what challenges people.

-Lord like a child I practice what challenges me, until I master them, turn your enemies into lovers so you can be who you are to them.

-Lord, I pray let me have a supernatural saturated abundance of healing oil for my mind, thoughts and heart, lord Jesus heal all the nations, lord heal the nations, heal in every place of their lives, heal every heart, mind, thoughts, souls, and bodies.

CHAPTER 6

The lord is good to all psalm 145:9 ~ healing the Nations

God Christ Jesus changed his mind from Matthew 18:3 to Matthew 18:4, all things are possible with God Jesus -mark 9:23,- Luke 18:27 he could have changes of his mind in the all things, the lord will bring fresh changes for his people, the lord he can and has the authority to change his mind over and over and over again because 1 Corinthians 13:4-8 says His love hopes all things for his people, endures all things for his people, believes all things for his people, and bears all things for his people, so why would God's people limit god Jesus and god the father in the all things. psalm 57:2 says, god most high performs all things, he will give you creative blessings in his word, creative new changes for his people and creative prayers to intercede for all people in the all things because we should not want to see people lost, God Jesus will do all things, so he is not limited to staying the same in the all things. Isaiah 43:18-19 says behold the lord will do a new thing for his people, he will give his people new heavenly names, and new heavenly identities, new blessings, new lifestyles, new miracles, new everything the lord is good to all, rich in mercy, he will bring his people new forgiveness, new grace, new mercy, new land, new hearts and new minds, new healings, new restored bodies, new life, new vision and new abundance if people want a relationship with God Jesus, all things are possible with God- Matthew 19:26. God Jesus will get creative in all things, and God's people can live in all things forever. He will go the distance being the god he wants to be, and just let him be God.

So what does it take for people to be childlike and walk in Godly humility to obtain the grace they desire to continue in a relationship with Christ Jesus it is becoming childlike. It is not after the glams and games of ministry, leaders who should not seek their own recognition and honor. People's hearts should only be for Christ Jesus only and not necessarily concerned about obtaining a self-honor for selfish gain and selfish pride in the heart and mind. None of those things should really matter when it comes to Christ Jesus, he brings those closer to him who just want him and only him Christ Jesus. That's what childlike faith is only wanting Christ Jesus first, and not people being so much within themselves because they walk with Christ Jesus longer than others have. Childlike faith it's to teach an older generation who hath been walking with Christ Jesus longer than little children who Jesus called over to him in Matthew 18:1-4. With pride and arrogance from his disciples he was willing that quick to give them up because he wanted his apostle's hearts to stop being only for themselves at heart only just because they were walking with Jesus closer than the little child. Leaders who walk with Jesus longer than children or even people does not make people closer to the lord or not it's the heart that makes people close to the lord. He told his disciples if they did not humble themselves like a child they would be without him in hell if they did not humble themselves like a child. Because Jesus loved his disciples and caught them because he loved them he said if they were to humble themselves like a child they would be the greatest in the kingdom of heaven. So, the more people humble themselves as a child in humility, I'm sure Christ Jesus has a greater grace for them. Humility brings in abundance of grace, gives you access to the kingdom of heaven, and saves the soul but by staying with Christ Jesus if many people seek that type of grace it's available to those who pursue the humilities of having a saving relationship with Christ Jesus, because remember we do everything in relationship with Christ Jesus as first, and never not leaderships and people only for themselves in ministries concerning their hearts is what Christ Jesus keeps his eyes on. I'm learning this just because leaderships want people's money. That does not mean those leaderships have your complete best interest in their hearts. So, Christ Jesus is teaching to look beyond their prophesying in faith-based books, Christian websites, and sermons of religious leaders, and social media and look at the heart from which these prophecies are coming from.

Just because they got the sounding good words on title sermons on these prophecies does not mean they got the love in their hearts to back it up. It's many leaders in wolves in sheeps clothes that can meet people right when they are in their relationship with God but their hearts are out to destroy people. - Mathew 4:1-12

Ephesians 6 says in the bible that there will be principalities and powers, rulers of darkness, and spiritual wickedness in high places that will speak to God's people and operate in many churches and in God's kingdoms but yet with principalities and powers speaking in these days churches and the deceptions of ministry, christ jesus divided the kingdoms of satan for yet for the blood of Christ Jesus to overrule principalities and powers. Who do come in the form of God in ministries but really wolves in sheeps clothings, heirlings and false prophets. Christ jesus said that principalities would go out into the world and deceive God's people and even the very elect because at heart they don't have God's people best interest at heart, but for their selfish gain and hidden agendas... but christ jesus said those who follow him will not be deceived by deception because he is light of the world, and that if we continue with him we are his disciples indeed we shall know the truth and the truth will make us free. -John 8:31-36

Christ Jesus told me how his leadership is doing? And he said pride and arrogance is making him lose his generals, prophets and God's people because of pride, selfish pride and selfish gain in his kingdom. So many people choose the pride of life over serving him from a place of relationship with him. He told me many of his generals and prophets and a generation of believers all have selfish gain in their hearts, how they leave their congregations sick in their bodies from cancer and diseases in their churches, leaderships not healing people like Christ Jesus healed people and God's people are crying out for healing in their bodies even when they leave church services. Christ Jesus told me that many people in congregations are being robbed from their heavenly names and heavenly identities, and how many leaders do not have a dream interpretation ministry in their churches and yet I see god's people perishing from lack of knowledge in this day's churches.

It's kind of like this says Christ Jesus if leaders are making money off God's people, then people eat from a knowledge that is not the knowledge of healing from God the father that Christ Jesus walked in. God the father's knowledge he's displeased. Instead of God's people eating the fruit of good and evil, that leaven bread won't hinder them from eating the fresher fruit that God had offered Adam and eve in the book of genesis 3 chapter before they both sinned, because they were not thankful for the fresher fruit that God originally offered them they settled for leaven bread type of fruit, that left Adam and Eve from enjoying the fresher presence of the lord. People are leaving their churches which symbolizes the garden of eden in the spirit realm without the presence of the lord concerning the fresher fruit because they eat so much of good and evil that is a reflection of leaven bread. So if God's people want the fresher presence of the lord they better watch what trees they eat from, because if God's people are being offered the leaven bread of fruit of good and evil from their teachers and leaderships then it could be they don't have the presence of the lord of the fresher fruit like they were offered by God originally.- Genesis 3 chapter. Their teachers and leadership are giving them that themselves fruit, instead of people enjoying a fresher presence of the lord and the fresher fruit of the lord. Their teachers and leadership should not give their congregations rotten fruit and call it God.

CHAPTER 7
Godly humility that routs pride and arrogance.

Lord lead your generals, believers, and leaderships in Godly wisdom and let me call a lost relative in my family that I have not talked to in a long time because they may not have people praying for them, why should I forsake mine lost love ones to get recognized by the rich or to serve the lord, why should I see them suffering in the spiritual realm and not call them, encourage them, and be a blessing to them. Matthew 18:1-4.

Lord heal this type of behavior in generals, believers, and and leaders From the consequences of hell Matthew 18:1-4 Christ Jesus did say if his followers did not humble themselves like a child they would not go to heaven, but those who humble themselves like a child would be the greatest in heaven. This means that only christ jesus could break his curse of hell off his followers if the proper humility was lived before him.
Lord Jesus, I ask that you heal the nations from the curse

of hell like you spoke to your apostles who followed you, Christ Jesus giving consequences of hell to his apostles and followers, but with love he was willing to break his curse if they learned humility. Christ Jesus said it but he changed his mind and took it away for those who would humble themselves like children. Matthew 18:3-4
Christ Jesus did curse his apostles from going to heaven not to go to heaven but it was by their choice if they did not learn humility like children

-Lord let leaders boast in your corrections putting them first so that they may obtain a greater humility in christ. -Matthew 18:1-4

-Lord Jesus let leaders, believers and generals be teachable like a child, never too old to learn new things. God is doing a new thing.- isaiah 43:18, - Matthew 18:3-4

-Lord let leaders and generals humble themselves greater than children do, put away childish things, give up their toys of ministry for something better in heaven. -luke 19

-Lord let not leaders and generals forsake children to get recognized by the rich people, children in ministries have needs to, they too need healing, encouragement, correction, and discipline. Matthew 18:1-4

-Lord let leaders and generals celebrate the children in their ministries and do not forsake their healing and personal needs to get recognized by the rich people. -Matthew 18:1-4

-Lord let people celebrate those around them, ask people they don't know much about if they need anything, in stores you can buy their food, or bless people around them just because. celebrate people around you, love those around you, and put love always first. -Matthew 18:1-4

-Lord let not leaders and generals forsake children in their congregations to serve the Lord let leaders spend time with the children of their ministries. -Matthew 18:1-4.

-Lord let leaders and generals spend time with their servants' children. -Matthew 18:1-4.

-Lord let leaders and believers humble themselves like a child and fear the lord. Matthew 18:1-3

-Lord let me remove anyone or anything that wants to take your place as first in my life. Matthew 18:1-4

-Lord let me put the needs of poor people first, let us do good to servants who do contribute to the faith in jesus name

-Lord let me make sacrifices from sinning in kingdom authority in jesus name

-Lord let generals, believers and leaders sacrifice the sinful wills of other leaders to put god almighty father first in Jesus name.

-Lord let generals, and leaders surrender their churches for a more enhanced life in Christ jesus in jesus name

-Lord let leaders and generals no longer yield to their members to be servants of unrighteousness. in Jesus name. -Romans 6:13

-Lord, seeing sin i sin not, hearing sin I think not. in jesus name

-Lord let leaders, people and generals see the true

condition of hearts and help struggling believers in Jesus' name.

-Lord let generals, leaders, and believers labor with those who are struggling to forgive people because they were hurt really badly in churches or relationships of the past, let them call up these people and giving encouragement, love to those who suffering, and tell them God's heart about how he is their strength to forgive those of their past they will humble themselves like children and make people feel better. -matthew 18:1-4

-Lord jesus let me give you a yes lord throughout my day, i wanna please you and honor you by obeying you, serving you until i die, praying that you be pleased with my faith, and reward those who diligently obey you in jesus name

-Lord Jesus, your commandments are sweet. I wanna know them for they are sweeter than my past lovers and greater than my family, it's not the ministry that takes people higher, it's a daily washed and cleansed heart and mind in Jesus name.

-Lord let leaders, people, generals keep a loving mindset towards people and God in Jesus name.

-Lord let leaders, generals, and people humble themselves like a child catching an enemy in the spirit realm in their time of need to restore them; they could not have their families praying for them nor helping them.

-Lord let leaders, generals, and people heal their loved ones from fetters, yokes, and mental illnesses, let men step up in families and protect their loved ones, let them humble themselves.

-Lord let generals, believers, and leaders win lost souls like it's people's last day to live.

-Lord let people see the true condition of an enemy's hearts and just be a blessing to them just because. lord let people do just because blessings for people around them.

-Lord let people stay honest and truthful with people all the time. in jesus name

-Lord let leaders, generals, and believers practice being there for people, not just on Sundays and bible study nights, it should be a daily thing.

-Lord let people bring changes to people's lives, let them intercede for the lost people.

-Lord let leaders, generals, and people practice what challenges them.

-Lord let leaders, generals, and people go out their way in ministry to check on their servants, or family, and friends.

-Lord let not leaderships do ministry from a place of their own selfish authority. Lord, I pray let them humble themselves like a child and use their authority childlike.

-Lord let leadership generals, people and humble themselves to help people as much as they ask.

Lord, I pray if leaders and generals have the power to do good, let them do good to people, let them humble themselves like children.

-Lord let generals and leaders listen to hurting people and bless them.

-Lord let me pray each day how can i humble myself and honor you lord in a special way, what pleases you lord that i should honor you this day and

the rest of my life, keep my heart and mind in your word.

-Lord, I pray let leaders accept it when people walk away from serving them any longer. Godly humility is this like a child when their servants walk away from them it was because their leadership was a hindrance to their servants and their servants saw that in their leaders. Do not curse them, do not condemn them like a child would not because they no longer want to serve under your leadership but like a child be humble let them go, let your servants walk away and keep interacting with those around you who will go the distance with you. Matthew 18:1-4

-God Jesus will test the hearts of many people concerning families. He does this to show us ourselves so he can change us and to look at our lost relatives in his eyes, people we do not know, people we do know through his childlike faith but around us. People never know they could have other family members who do not care to pray for them and do not want to see them do anything with their lives. Yet they want what they see in their relatives destinies, this is the selfish gain that is seen in many leaderships, in families, communities and people. People must humble themselves as a child to do something about their lost relatives, people they do know and don't know why forsake your loved ones to get recognized by the rich and recognized by their enemies. Matthew 18:1-4. Lord, I pray they heal lost families from hell.

-Never forsake an enemy to get recognized by the rich, be ready to pray for them if they are dying and sick. Humble yourself like a child, restore them, and keep it moving. visit them in the hospitals, prisons, and in the communities. See how they are doing? This is humility I have practiced when it was serving the lord in street ministry. I was Visiting my brother in Christ in prison, going to elderly people's rooms and praying for them and they were enemies of the past in the spirit realm. Honoring enemies on the streets with Jesus' love.

-God Jesus says there will be many false leaderships who are false prophets who got the book titles, Christian websites, internet, social media, or major platforms, and sermons they got the titles of these things but don't have the love behind their titles to back up their faith and love for people, lord I pray heal false teachers, and heal false prophets from hell, lord heal them and sit them down for deliverance to learn humility. Lord, I pray for a special protection on new believers for what they hear, and they need to learn how to hear from you, then from false teachers and prophets of the gospel who don't have their best interest at heart..

-Never watch your enemies struggle in the spirit realm, humble yourself like a child and love your enemies, don't be afraid to honor people and they really don't deserve it. This is humility and what a child would do, without concerning themselves at heart if people like them or not. Call your enemies if you got their number and be kind to them. This is the gospel of Christ we Gotta love our enemies, how can we bring change to those who don't like us, what reward have ye?

-Lord let not leaders, generals, and believers forsake the poor to get recognized by the rich, why should people forsake them, they have little money, and are in poverty and impoverished people. Forsaking the poor gains nothing but pride and arrogance, someone said this that the poor are as important to God as the rich. The bible says in proverbs 2:22 that the poor and the rich meet together; the lord is the maker of them all. Why forsake people who do not have as much you as you do, this day lord Jesus make people accountable for doing something from a place they already have for homeless people, impoverished and sick people in their churches, in their families, and in their communities.-Matthew 18:1-4

-Lord let leaders and prophets, and teachers not use congregation money to buy them a new car or house and they do not plan on serving the lord with it or healing the sick in their churches. Lord Jesus check their motives to why they all want a major platform and why it's not really needed in your relationship with them. They must know that as long as they have Godly love they can do anything through Christ Jesus who strengthens them. Major platforms not needed. Philippians 4:13, Matthew 18:1-4, why should they misuse congregation money and people come to their ministries impoverished and sick in their bodies. leaders are accountable for every lost soul in their ministries and the sick who are left unhealed in their churches.

-Lord let not generals, leaders, and believers of big ministries let them not buy them another car, or house that are sick, poor, and impoverished people in their churches. they could be using those things to serve the lord, using their visionary skills for lost souls on the streets and out working the Lord's kingdom, and not locating women to sleep with already married women for adultery.

-Lord let not your leaderships and people forsake their enemies to get recognized by the rich, lord Jesus you told us in Matthew 5:44 to love our enemies, bless them that curse them, and do good to people, pray for those people who do not like you, and humble themselves as a child doing it by the heart because we got to want the best interest for those people who do not like you. Christ Jesus instructed us to love our enemies because we may not like their sins but we still got to love them and want their best interest at heart, if you see them sick do good to them, visit them in the hospitals, do good to your enemies even if they be your family members, look in the mirror and make that change, because sometimes the lord can see things in them that he wants to use for his Glory if he knows it will bring him the honor it's well worth it from the lord to invest love for his Glory. -Matthew 18:1-4

-Lord Never let people misjudge people through the eyes of other leaders, get to know people's hearts before you pass a judgement and God Jesus did not speak. God Jesus can heal anyone, heal anything and redeem anything. Lord, I pray let leaders, generals, and believers humble themselves like a child in this area.

-Lord, I pray let leaders, generals, and prophets get to know people's hearts first without misjudging them. I do not like the Pharisees that did not want to know Jesus' heart for people of justice and mercy he had done miracles for. More leaders should save lives than leaders thinking they can put people in a hell when those leaders deserve the same place, who are leaders to judge they deserve the same hell they want for others unless they repent and walk in love.-repent

-Never misjudge people or pass a judgement over people's lives to fit in with other people and want to be recognized by the rich. In Matthew 7:1-2 Christ Jesus said judge not that ye be not judged for with what measure people judge others it will be measured back onto them. Luke 6:37 Christ Jesus says judge not that ye be not judged, condemn not and ye be not condemned. Forgive and ye shall be forgiven.

-Lord let me see the true condition of my enemies and not forsake them to get recognized by the rich, why should we forsake people who have something against us in their hearts, Christ Jesus the changer of hearts concerning enemies, some-times people may want to get rid of their enemies but we got to love them as well but having their best interest at heart. Matthew 18:1-4

-Lord let me preserve the destiny of my enemies because so did you when you died for all people on the cross over 2,000 years ago you were right there with them when you died for their sins. lord Let me be trusted with the destiny of my enemies, because God may not want us to hurt them, but make a difference in their lives to bring them closer to God in heart, and for their healing. Lord let me never forsake an enemy to get recognized by the rich. We must humble ourselves as a child and have the best interest for our enemies at heart, it's what Christ Jesus would do even though we do not like their sins. Matthew 18:1-4.

-Lord let me have the king Melchizedek anointing (genesis 14:18-20) where I am trusted with the souls of your Abrahams and will NOT rob from them in Godly prophecy to get to them to the next level of God's promises, lord I know if I give them their destinies you will historically count it as righteousness and honor those who had believed in the legacies of your Abrahams. and faith patriarchs of the gospel. That if I am used by God the father to promote kings their destinies are preserved in my spirit and I am trusted by the lord to daily promote kings because they could be greater in God's promises than I am, I dare NOT be jealous of them in my heart and not promote them. -Matthew 18:1-4. someone said" give a king his wealth in faith believing for them and the nations from all around them wherever they go are restored because of the fresh presence of the lord upon their lives."

-Lord I humble myself like a child and ask for a fresh protection over the lives of new believers on milk so they won't be taken advantage of by false leaders who are bishops and teachers of the gospel in churches, so other young women won't be taken into adultery, and young men will not be killed by the David and Saul spirit that take wives from other men to kill other men who are Glory carriers like Uriah the Hittite.

-Lord let me catch my enemies in the spirit realm and in their time of need restore them, because I should care about their needs first than my own personal ambitions or selfish desires, we got to put people first than ourselves, sometimes God will surround us with our enemies to see what we would do but God knowing he will protect us before them. It will be to see how willing we are to be selfless from that place of his cross for them over 2,000 years ago, not an easy prayer but we got to live this gospel like it's our last day to live, and people's last day to repent.

God the father says I need more generals and leadership to repent like it's their last day to live, they only win lost souls in their churches why should they go to heaven? when people watch for leaders to come to them.

-Lord, I pray let generals, leaders, and believers win lost souls around them like it's their last to live and repent, for their families, and people around them. Be a blessing to people around you. you could see lost souls walking the streets and God could want you to pray for them, God's prayer for them through you could be their last chance to repent. That's what God wants in soul winners.

God the father says i have too many murderers, adulterers, and whores leading my kingdoms they will be judged harshly, jesus teaches love not murder and iniquity, their will be judgement for how my sons run my kingdom, i must judge because its my authority and perfect will to judge men who lie and take lives i love. Let's get to know people who do contribute to the gospel or ministries will remain to me like dung.

CHAPTER 8
A personal Reflection

When I was serving the lord in nursing homes, I met elderly people who families forsook them, I was the last person to pray for them and get them covered underneath Christ Jesus blood of atonement because they were dying, because those elderly people did not know anything that, and they were very sick with dementia and Alzheimer's. I was the last person to pray and intercede for them all before they all died when I left that job to go to another one, and came back to the same job they were all dead of those I prayed for. Sometimes people out in the communities and jobs don't even got their own families praying for them. Maybe a love prayer of intercession for people they could do if they see they don't got their families praying for them just like they met the elderly people. Those elderly people were so sick they did not know about repenting, their minds gone from them. Those elderly people were poor, and their families forsook them. God almighty father used me to save over 50

elderly people at my past job and be their bridge to heaven because their minds did not have jesus, and when they were dying i was in position to cover them with the blood of jesus and get them all in heaven, where their families did not believe in prayer for them, and they were given medicine but the medicine was not working for those elderly people who were dying. Those elderly people did not know when they would die, but the lord did and he sent me to cover them and I did for the glory of God and his honor.

Lord I pray that leaders, generals, and believers would use their authority to save lives rather than take lives, that they would use their authority to make a difference in people's lives instead of misjudging them. let's get to know the many people in God's kingdoms instead of people looking through the eyes of leaders that misjudge those who are innocent in God's eyes because he changed them.

-Lord let not leaderships misjudge those who are repentant in heart and who do obey you and are of the household of faith, lord let leaderships be accountable for every soul they could have saved and covered them underneath Christ Jesus blood of atonement. Matthew 18:1-4, lord rebuke them all for selfish gain in authority that's a serious pride problem and issues of this day's leaderships including a generation of believers.

-Lord, let me stay honest and truthful with you and people all the time. If we are from God the father, we will know the Godly truth and speak the Godly truth. One thing that God the father can't stand is lies that are concealed, and people do not humble themselves and undo them, people tell lies they better be prepared to undo them. The bible says in psalm 120:2. God will deliver people from lying tongues, repent

-Lord let not major platforms rob leaderships from going to heaven, leaderships and people will not use them to seek their own honor but they will humble themselves and put away their major platforms that are a pride and arrogance addiction, nobody said your relationship with God Jesus had to be lived from major platforms to major platforms if we do not have Godly love to back up what we preach than the major platforms mean nothing to Christ Jesus 1 Corinthians 13 chapter prophecies will cease, and become nothing unto the lord

-When I was working at the nursing home, a former job before I had to quit, I remember Christ Jesus' word came to me in my car and he said why forsake elderly people who do not know how to pray for themselves to get recognized by the rich? Now you humble yourself like a child, be willing to help them and pray for them to move in action, let them know they are not forgotten and I love them and cover them underneath my blood of atonement, and pray for them concerning eternity with me to be a bridge to them. Jesus' heart says this. Why should leaders and believers forsake people who need them the most to get recognized by the rich. There are leaders and believers who are putting their sinful selfish desires first before the true condition of people. Jesus said to me sick did you visit me. -Matthew 25:36 and I obeyed Christ Jesus went to all the elderly sick people at my former job and I lived what Jesus told me to do Christ Jesus gives grace to those who humble themselves. -Matthew 18:4.

-Lord let not generals, leaders, and believers not forsake people who cannot do for themselves. Matthew 18:1-4, there are sick people who come to their churches who don't even know how to say a prayer to help themselves, yet many leaders, generals, and believers are enriching themselves, and these sick people in their congregations are leaving the same way they came. Many Leaders must do some serious sitting down for deliverance from pride and arrogance. And watch what they put first in ministry and relationship with Christ Jesus or they could be lost for the deceitfulness of riches in Christ Jesus eyes. -Mark 4:19

-Lord if I am humble then cause me to continue to humble myself like a child. The humble are still teachable just like a small child is. - Psalm 25: 9-14. Lord, I am dependent and trusting like a child knowing that you will take care of me, you will teach me like a child would seek I humble myself lord. Lord make me a lover of you lord with my heart and mind like a child does. A child thinks the best thoughts about Jesus if you teach them at young ages, they just want to know more about Jesus Matthew 18:1-4 they want a relationship with Jesus, they should Not be imitators of unrighteousness like they see in adults. -3 john 1:11

-Lord, I pray let me teach my children how to humble themselves, they are already young and teachable and will listen, let us teach our children how NOT to be influenced by ungodly teachers of the gospel.

-Lord let me humble myself like a child and pray for people who do not know how to pray for themselves, lord if I know anybody who may be sick, elderly, disabled, or an undesirable of society lord let me pray for them and give them your heart's best interest at my heart and care for them and all things you lead me to do for them to honor you Christ Jesus, I humble myself like a child. Lord I ask that you bless me to keep being a blessing to those around me even to those who do not like me in their hearts -Matthew 18:1-4

-Lord, I pray to show me what enemy I can bless to honor you this day and we keep it only between you and me to honor you lord in our relationship because my recognition comes from you lord Jesus, and not necessarily from people. What pleases your heart lord this day? And what can I do for you lord this day? How can I bring honor to you this day lord for your Glory I humble myself like a child and give you a yes lord?

-Lord, I pray what's on your heart for people that I may honor them this day? I humble myself like a child.

-Lord, I pray to fill me up with just because blessings to do for people around me this day, and how can I humble myself like a child and serve them uprightly as if I'm doing this unto you lord just between me and you I don't have to be recognized to serve you?

-Lord, I pray that I can humble myself like a child to serve you each and every day without any lip on where I should go? What should I do?, or what to say I'll just give you a yes lord.

-Lord, I pray that I will be a blessing to those around me on this day? Who's on your heart to serve in the streets lord I humble myself like a child. -Matthew 18:4

-Lord, I pray today that you use my authority to bless those who are deemed less in authority by others. I humble myself like a child in the way I use kingdom authority. lord I honor you, i love you jesus, and I only want you.

-Lord, who can I forgive that trespassed against me this day? How can I humble myself like a child and bless them without expecting anything in return. May the heavenly father deliver me from the power of evil.- Matthew 6:14-15

-Lord, I pray that I can love my enemies this day to honor you? Who can I bless just because I'm not too busy with ministry work to serve you, not forsaking those who you send me to that you showed me in the spirit realm.

-Lord, I pray that the homeless people I can feed this day and get them a job in my business or church. How can I use what I already have to be a blessing to people I don't know that you have already given me? How can I humble myself like a child and share my blessings with other people?

-Lord, I pray that leadership and believers will choose to show people the sincere love of God, without them being crooked minded and crooked hearted towards people. Lord, we humble ourselves like a child. How can leadership, generals, and believers be a blessing to people who do not have major platforms like they do, or are not popular with titles, or high positions in God's kingdom. The first will be last and the last first. -Matthew 19:30

-Lord let me see in you in the eyes of children that is it not those who have major platforms and high positions of popularity in the gospel who are close to you in heart, but those they deem less in authority to them.

-Matthew 18:1-4, a people would draw near to the lord with their lips and their hearts be far from him. -Matthew 15:8-12

-Lord let me love you with all my heart, soul, and mind. -Matthew 22:37-40

-Lord you love me, more than what I can love you, you just love me despite of me you perfect those things that concern me. Psalm 138:8

-Lord, I pray that I will love you and love people in jesus name

-Lord, I pray you give me love in my heart and mind, you will take out stony hearts and replace them with love hearts. -Ezekiel 11:14-21.

-Lord, pour out divine supernatural saturations of the anointing of love on all people's hearts and minds, that place where we should serve you uprightly in relationship and ministry?

-Lord let divine healing heal all hearts and minds, lord all people need Godly love.

-Lord, let love and rebuke be given to those who hinder the love of God from other people, so they will be strongly convicted to let the love of God have free reign in the hearts and lives of others, even those they look down on.

-Lord, I pray, heal all birthdays, numbers, and heal the time, supernaturally saturate and cover it with the blood of Christ Jesus.

-Lord, I pray daily to restore my mind, redeem my thoughts, and heart.-Psalm 51 create in me a clean heart and renew in me the right spirit. Renew the right spirit in me to live right from my heart and mind.

-Lord, let not your leadership misjudge people who need God's love, who are leaders to restrict the love of God from hurting people. They may not know that those people really could have no one praying for them. Could need the love of God and Godly encouragement.

-Lord, I pray let me have a Godly love heart like you, I ask you to love lord Jesus, love me lord Jesus where I hurt in my heart, and redeem my thoughts and keep them covered underneath your blood of atonement.

-Lord let greater condemnation come upon those who teach -James 3:1-12 let all ungodly teachers and leaderships of the gospel be judged by the lord, let them sit down for deliverance because of pride and arrogance to find mercy.

-Lord let me humble myself greater than children and win lost souls for your kingdom any way I can that you lead me lord, because I choose to be teachable following you Jesus, you change my ways lord Jesus, so others can see how you changed me in my relationship with you.

-Lord, I pray let me not do ministry first over my relationship with you.

-The bible says many false prophets are in the world- lord let me have discernment on which prophecies to put first and which ones not to read help me see beyond what leaderships are prophesying to see the motives of their hearts and do they have God's best interest for people at heart or do their hearts want selfish gain in authority in ministry- Matthew 24:11

-Lord let leaderships and believers have the best interest at heart for all people, God Jesus give them a heart for all people if they serve in your kingdoms, leaderships and believers should not do ministry as workers of iniquity. Matthew 7:21-23

-Lord Jesus, I pray let me humble myself like a child so I can be humble and always humble myself so I can stay teachable underneath your divine authority over me. Sin undone in your name lord.

Lord someone said this "teachers must be teachable or else how would they learn more from other people than just by their head knowledge, and have a sour heart."

-False prophecies cease with God because the love was not real from the heart. People were jealous and selfish at heart. That's why they wanted to prophesy in people's lives because they wanted to use their major platforms to be a hindrance rather than walking in love. They just wanted God for their prophecies to come to pass and love not truly in their hearts though they called it love. Their motives were to fit in with other people, and not see people have God's promises because of jealousy and envy in their hearts against you.

Godly wisdom says this: Get by yourself with God for many seasons or even years to learn to turn everything off and hear from God yourself. Know God for only yourself. God's people got to watch who they listen to and who they follow as first, there are way too many leaders who are wolves in sheep's clothing in these end times in God's kingdoms. Not everyone who comes in Jesus' name is really for you at their heart; they could sound just like god in preaching or teaching, and they really are principalities of deception who come in the Lord's name.. Your teachers and leadership could be concealing something and want you to keep serving them as a distraction from you getting the real promises of God. Your teachers and leadership could be robbing you in heavenly identities and heavenly names, dream interpretations, and financially. Don't be a part of leadership that is lying in their giving to their congregations be different from what you see in churches and know God for yourself if you only put him first and keep him first.

I have seen leaders of deception from my youth on up, they speak in God's name, and preach in God's name, they do ministry in God's name but they are murderers, adulterers, bisexual jezebel women, evil minded leaderships, false prophets, and wolves in sheep's clothing, and they serve satan, and powers, demons they serve, and use other people to do their dirty work. The bible says these types of spirits will speak to people on major platforms and people will be deceived if it's God jesus. There are some dirty crooked criminal preachers who preach murder and discord on major platforms, preachers who murder, and steal from God's people in God's promises, steal their heavenly identities, and heavenly names. I've seen prayer intercessors who are murderers at heart, and hypocrisy. judgemental preachers who are nothing but money hungry, principalities who use God's truth for deception in ministry. satan has used his preachers and leaders to infiltrate God's kingdom in the churches in which is the spirit of deception. These days not too many genuine preachers.

-Lord let sin be purged from hearts and thoughts in my relationship with you, lord purge and purify and cleanse daily the sin of people's minds and hearts.

-God's people are being lied to from their teachers giving, they give routine sunday to sunday head knowledge, but God's people are being lied to in their healing from their teachers lying in their giving concerning healing this is going on in the churches.

-Lord, let not another leader or believer go to hell for pride and arrogance. Lord Jesus heal them with this book of prayers. I honor you Christ Jesus between you and me. I honor you. Major platforms, popularity, followers, and titles have become dark addictions and habits of many teachers leaders, and they have not confessed this sin to their congregations. Generals, prophets, teachers lost with titles - Matthew 18:1-3 humility says I will honor my congregation without holding them back from healing in their bodies because of just the head knowledge I want to preach. I will call people up who are suffering in my congregations to honor them, support them, and invest in their dreams like they invest in their churches teachers' sermons

Reflection: I had made a promise to Jesus by the rose bush that I wanted people to know his heart. I've kept my promise to him through this book and I've honored my lord jesus. because he wants people to know his heart, not just his name.

-Lord how many churches leaders and generals are willing to invest in the dreams of those suffering for Christ Jesus' sake in their churches.

-Lord let leaders and believers intercede for people who are lost, hoping that your heart for lost people will lead them to repentance and grace and mercy given.

-Lord, I pray to keep me restored unto repentance. You would that none perish but all come to repentance. -2 peter 3:9

-Lord, I pray when I see the true condition of an enemy in the spirit realm let me humble myself like a child and be a blessing to them, lord let me be kind and good to them because I have the power to do good, as leaders and believers we must do good to people when we have the power to. We really should humble ourselves like a child and do good to others NOT only on holidays, birthdays, or special events in churches, families, and communities. Honor and Celebrate people around you as a blessing. Like a child I do not have to know them to bless them just be kind to them to honor Christ Jesus in everything just between me and him.

-Lord Jesus, I ask who could I celebrate today and honor them that I do not know or know I humble myself greater than a child?

-Lord who could I honor today that will please you because my heart is to obey you in things between me and you, lord I don't have to get recognized by the rich to obey you because you love me.

-Lord let me celebrate a lost loved one in families to bring them closer to Christ Jesus and get them saved and redeemed.

-Lord, I pray let every general, leadership, and believers be accountable for every lost soul you told them to pray for around them and intercede for them, and they did not because of their motives to hinder the lord from using them.

-Take time out of your busy day of ministry each day and Celebrate Christ Jesus every day he died for all your sins. Lord, I pray I'll humble myself even when I can't humble myself any more than what I have personally between me and you. I will still humble myself like a child just to give you the glory lord.

-Lord Jesus let me celebrate you by winning lost souls like you do, I can celebrate you in my heart and in action, Passover day should not be the only day we celebrate Christ Jesus. Everyday, we should celebrate Christ Jesus in the way he puts it on your heart and your mind.

-God Jesus I ask for you to protect my labor for you and purify my oil over my labor because it is to you honor Christ Jesus, those who do not serve and labor in the kingdom of God could be without you even though you went out to greet them all.-Matthew 25: 1-13, -Matthew 18:1-4.

-Lord let my oil be healed and blessed by your presence Jesus, I labor to honor you lord Jesus, my healed oil has been pressed out in the field, lord Jesus I ask that you bless my labor only between me and you.

-Lord let your people be protected me from death and destruction, heal minds and hearts of its sins against you we confess, I humble myself as like a child you love me Jesus don't let me go of me lord Jesus when I'm wrong and guilty of my sins, lord I pray like a child love me despite if I'm wrong, and i'll do better next time when you show me how to make right choices and decisions the right way I humble myself like a child because you love me.

-Lord, let not your generals and leadership be without you because many serve you in the pride of life. Matthew 4 chapter, Luke 4 chapter.

-Lord let us see your generals, prophets, and believers healed from the consequences of hell because of sinful pride and arrogance. Lord, you hate pride.

-Lord let generals, leaders, and believers see why the pride of life hinders God's people from their divine healings in their congregations.

Holy father, I pray that your generals and leadership be not afraid to give up their churches to have a heavenly kingdom from you, and not the pride of life in Jesus name.

-Lord let my mind and thoughts be healed and cleansed daily, lord I confess many people need to change the way they think, lord heal our minds and condemning thoughts, you see us through Christ Jesus' blood of atonement over 2,000 years ago.

-Lord again let all people be healed from hell if they repent. Lord heal anything, lord heal all people, I pray and ask.

-Proverbs 8:13 says to fear the lord is to hate evil, I hate pride and arrogance, evil behavior and perverse speech.

-Proverbs 11:2 says when pride comes, then comes disgrace,

but with humility comes wisdom, proverbs 16:5 the lord detest all people perverse and proud at heart.

-The pride of life generals, believers, and leaderships without the father In 1 john 2:16-17 says for all that is in the world, the lust of the flesh, and the lust of the eyes, and the pride of life, is not from the father but is of the world. And the world passes away, and the lust thereof, but he that doeth the will of God abides forever.

-Father forgive them for operating in a worldly kingdom not of you holy father, forgive them but judge them. Lord judge, judge all your people, judge your leaderships and generals lord judge all unbelievers and let it be clear, and you judge holy father your all your people in your kingdoms.

-Father in Jesus name, let not your generals, leaderships, and believers be without you because of what 1 John 2:16-17 says lord heal them from hell, if they repent and obey Christ Jesus. Your word says lord you will redeem the souls of your servants- psalm 34:22, romans 8:28 says God redeems all things, redeems all people from their iniquities, missteps, and afflictions. God redeems the repentant from sin. I humble myself like a child, I should not put sin first before the authority of the lord.

-Lord, I pray let people humble themselves in their minds. More healing for minds and hearts. Lord daily healing from hell. We should humble ourselves like a child.

-The lord humbly will restore and reconcile unto himself all things, he will restore himself what he lost from you.-Colossians 1:20 the lord will have a change of mind.

-The lord will heal your sins, heal minds and thoughts he will take your sins away and bring you back unto him. For all things are possible with God. Matthew 19:26.

-He will have a change of mind that he shouldn't have let

you go because he will remember his love for you, and bring you back unto him, you will be his again.

-Lord, I prophesy to you, then let what you lost be brought back into your love. Lord bring all things back into your love, and love on people lord, the lord will reconcile my soul back to him, he will reverse his condemnation he spoke, the lord will have a change of mind and a change of heart, that you should be his once again. For all things are possible with God. -Matthew 19:26

-The Lord Jesus will heal God's people from death and hell. Matthew 19:26 all things are possible with God. He will heal people from condemnation and judgements for all things are possible with God. Matthew 19:26.

The lord will take away your suffering and struggles. For all things are possible with God. -Matthew 19:26

The lord will bless his people where he cursed them. For all things are possible with God. -Matthew 19:26

The lord will heal people's names, their reputations and influence, the lord will heal people from their demons. For all things are possible with God. Matthew 19:26

The lord will invade the psych wards and hospitals with supernatural Saturated healings for people for all things are possible with God. Matthew 19:26

CHAPTER 9

Praise God the father folks, celebrate God Jesus saints.

A JUST BECAUSE NATIONAL WEEK

Come on people I'm prophesying over your life will you believe in creative prophetic changing wills, shifting wills, prophetic changes, mind and heart changes from the lord.-Matthew 19:26 all things are possible with God. When are God's churches pew sitters gone let God bring creativity in lives. I've learned to base my worship on my heart for God in living obedience, and not just sermons.

The lord will redeem souls from his unforgiveness. He will heal all the nations from hell. -Colossians 3:10,-all things are possible with God. Matthew 19:16-26. just because blessings from God Jesus in all things. Lord Jesus supernaturally saturate this country with healing love.

God Jesus will do all things; he will turn people called of the devil into divine deliverers for all things are possible with God. -Matthew 19: 26 He will turn evil people into evolutionists. For all things are possible with God he will save the souls who other people did not want to see saved, that's why we celebrate him not just on Passover day we celebrate Christ Jesus every day, he will heal all the nations from hell because all things are possible with God, God Jesus will do more healing bringing love, love, love into people's hearts and minds. For all things are possible, he will restore lost souls.

-Lord let none of those who take refuge in you, will not be punished. psalm 32:22

-The lord will redeem the souls of his servants- psalm 34:22

- Lord, I pray let everything will be redeemed. For the lord is plenteous in redemption. -Psalm 130:7-8.

- Lord redeems all people if they repent and put Christ Jesus atonement first over 2,000 years ago.

-Lord let me be willing to give up big churches just to have the heavenly kingdom from the holy father.- Matthew 18:1-4

-Lord we are just preaching but what about the manifest power of Christ Jesus walked in where the manifestation was from God the Father as his source and not people's pockets.

-Lord again heal your generals, leaderships, and people, unbelievers from hell, lord I pray for them. I intercede for them lord heal all your people from hell and heal the land of which they ask for.

-proverbs 16:18-20 says pride goes before destruction. Lord, heal your generals, leaderships, and believers from sinful pride and arrogance lord save them despite themselves you love them lord and do not want to see them lost for pride and arrogance. You would not that any perish but all come to repentance 2 peter 3:9

-Lord let not pride and arrogance be the reason people lose their souls, because of world popularity and their major platforms are a curse to their own selfish ambitions and selfish desires of having a relationship with God Jesus.

-Lord, let me have wisdom that comes with humility.

-Lord, let me humble myself in humility let me keep humbling myself like a child, break me lord in humility, lord I pray break evil minds in your humility. Break all evil minds of adultery, deception, and murder off of leadership mindsets. Lord, I pray that you humble their minds if they don't humble themselves.

-Lord, I pray that I be trusted with my enemies' hearts and minds.

-Lord, when I humble myself you lift me up, I humble myself like a child -James 4:10. Matthew 18:1-4.

-Lord let people put the needs of hurting people first instead of any selfish desires on major platform for themselves-Philippians 2:3

-Lord let not your leaderships, generals, and believers rob from you in honor-Matthew 18:3.

-Lord Proverbs 18:2 says before a downfall the heart is haughty, with humility comes before honor.

-Lord, let my conscience be healed, cleansed and restored daily, new thoughts I ask daily, and daily restore my soul.

-Lord let not leaderships and people sin with their hearts and minds to live like that. Lord, let them humble themselves like a child and daily clean their hearts and minds if they want that but you teach them to decide if they will be clean or unclean in their relationship with you. lord, you would want daily cleansing to cleanliness.

-Lord, let me cleanse me from evil, and protect me through Christ Jesus' blood of atonement over 2,000 years ago… God's love conquers evil. He heals all things, bears all things, hopes all things. The enduring healing of the lord

-Lord let all your people be healed from hell, lord rescue your people. You sent your word and healed your people from their destruction psalm 107:20

-Lord let leaders and believers humble themselves like a child. They do not have the authority on earth to put people in a hell and they deserve that same place for themselves, Christ Jesus died for all.

-Lord, let me stay repentant in heart that I might find grace if I choose to daily repent and let you change me God Jesus, there is a grace for the saints and sinners, a grace that comes from Christ Jesus atonement over 2,000 years ago.

-Lord let leaders and believers bow their hearts and minds at the feet of your cross over 2,000 years ago, you died for our sins, and we humble ourselves like a child for the grace we would seek from you to inherit the kingdom of heaven.

-Lord let not what people think what people say to them

-Lord if you gave me the power to trample over scorpions and all the power of the enemy, then lord let me humble myself as a child and be used to bring change to others and be the change you want to see in others I just want to be used by you lord Jesus because you love me and chose me and called me closer to you. Matthew 18:1-4.

-Lord, I pray thank you for your enduring healing for all the nations, the type of enduring healing in every situation and circumstance, for people who don't know you and those who do. All things are healed by your love, great almighty father, thank you lord for love and healing. All things are possible at the end of everybody's lives. -Matthew 19:26

-The blood of Christ Jesus against the curse of hell in all the nations. All things are possible with God. Matthew 19:26

-Lord Jesus delivers us from the father's wrath to come. - 1 thessalonians 4:11

-Lord let me win lost souls like it's their last day to live and repent. Lord, let my steps be ordered to those I can pray for, let me be a blessing to those people around me who God tells me they are lost, who knows I could be the last person who prays for them. That is how consistent God's leadership and God's people should be winning lost souls. We do not change people, God Jesus does that. I must love my neighbor as myself. - Matthew 22:37-39. I'll love all those around me.

-Lord many leaderships and people do not have to be seen on tv, social media, or Christian websites loving those around them. Ministry work does not always need tv or to be seen. Lost souls need love in restaurants, gas stations, stores, those who walk the streets, lost relatives, in banks, at parks, drive thru lines, jails, psych wards, and hospitals. What about them loving those around them on the streets and in those places.

-Lord let me do something just because for the people around me, that comes from my heart, and I do not have to be recognized by others to do it but recognized by you lord. Matthew 18:1-4 the small child Jesus called to him was recognized by Jesus, and not recognized by his apostles until Jesus corrected their faith to change their hearts, not their position.

-Lord let me not seek my own honor in a relationship with you, I will put you first than selfish desires of the heart, relationship with you comes first than what I gain from the congregations of the ministry. Matthew 18:1-4

-Lord, let me bless people just because God loves all people. -psalm 144:15, no matter who people are, they are all loved by God, lord I humble myself like a child and ask you to heal all the nations. Lord, I pray to serve those in ministry and who have a relationship with you who have served you uprightly and been your answered prayer and NOT ever your hindrance lord.

Word of the lord
The lord says:
-I need new leadership who will NOT be my hindrance when it comes to my kingdom work and have all people's best interests at heart. I want my leadership to learn how to see all people through Christ Jesus' blood, his redemptive work that I honor

in all lives who I know will do what I need them to do when it comes to lost souls around them.

-Lord let me serve you like a child; I humble myself like a child. I'll love all people regardless of what they look like, what they have or don't have, I'll humble myself like a child and give to people not only on birthdays, holidays or special events. I'll celebrate people I don't know or do everyday -Matthew 18:1-4

-When was the last time leadership and people celebrated their family members not just on their birthdays just because they are loved by God, humble yourself like a child.

-Lord let your generals and leaders celebrate and honor their servants, it's not just about the work they want their servants to do for them. Leaders should never condemn or talk badly about their servants then those leaders' ministries could lose people who no longer want to serve them.

-Lord heal your word for the healing of all the nations, if we have sinned against you lord, then I pray to heal all our sins. Lord, we pray we humble ourselves like a child.

Word of the lord
The lord says:
In these last days I'm seeing too much of the false prophetic being in churches, and in my kingdoms and churches. Nothing false has authority in my kingdom, no falsehood gets its way with me, you want your prophecies blessed by me then love people from your hearts, and not tell people you love them falsely, and curse them, exploit them, and shame them to fit in with other people. No false prophecies will I breathe on neither rest my presence upon it to make your prophecies not come to pass even if you want everybody to say it. I God the father will change all

false prophetic wills and prophecies until I see a generation of leaderships that will love people and NOT hinder my work with them. You hinder my work, I God the father hinder your prophecies. Prophecies shall cease without love – 1corinthians 13;8-10

The lord God the father says had people loved they would NOT have been murderers, adulterers, and thieves and they say they love my people and think they preach a love gospel, their false prophecies i speak of a crop failure.

The word of the lord
The lord says:
What makes my leaderships pass judgements on others because they judge people through the eyes of others, who is the judge? I thought Christ Jesus died for all. So why prophesy judgements and don't humble yourselves to go through what my leaderships are putting people through who are deemed less in authority to them, but not to me. Who told my leadership to judge, and I have not spoken to them, is not Christ Jesus' blood sufficient for all people, he came to love and do good, so what makes my leadership exempt because they exploited others for selfish gain and lies. Putting burdens on them they can't carry by themselves and using your major platforms to spread discord and hurt others I have loved with my heart. Why should I let my leadership in my kingdom of heaven, my leaderships have been showing the world a false image of love. I see nothing but selfishness in the way my leaders are using their authority, and they wont open their hardened hearts

and see all people through the blood of Christ Jesus over 2,000 years ago. Therefore, it is the lord God of Abraham, Issac, and Jacob who shall judge all my leaderships and that is my judgement that all false prophecies given to hinder my work in my people's lives will be hindered by me God the father, until my prophets have the least of mine best interest at their hearts.

-I humbled myself like a child and give what I already have from my heart to people. Lord, I pray I humble myself like a child and see people like they do. I'll humble myself like a child. -Matthew 18:1-4

-Lord, how does your heart want me to serve you on this day? Does not always have to be in the churches, what is your heart lord Jesus for someone around me this day i'll humble myself like a child? guide me to people who want me to come in their path or their direction.

-Lord, I'll give you a daily yes lord from my heart, I'll humble myself like a child without questioning you lord I'll be your answered prayer without hindering you in ministry. I'll be used like a child in ministry and relationship with you, and ill know how to stand before you lord humbling myself, when it comes to others. -Matthew 18:1-4

-Lord, if i'm driving and see homeless people asking and begging for food or what they may need, let me stop driving and serve them, let me go out of my way to bless them.

-Lord let not your leaderships be the cause of you losing souls, lord again let them NOT be your hindrance in ministry, lord you don't want to lose souls because of the sins of leaderships, this I pray a special prayer for all people who were forced to sin by leaders to be healed in all the nations from hell, and their souls restored established.- psalm 23:1-5

-Lord let me have faith like a child would you let me see through their eyes- Matthew 18:1-4

-Lord, let me have faith in you just like a child does. Matthew 18:1-4

-Lord let me love those around me no matter what they look like to me. In my thoughts I humble myself like a child's love thoughts for people. Matthew 18:1-4 Man looks at the appearance God looks at the heart. 1 Samuel 16:7

-Lord let me keep my thoughts as like a small child would about all people. -Matthew 18:1-4, lord let all people humble their minds like a child. It's the Lord who establishes humility in our minds and thoughts. This is repentance to let Jesus change our thinking.

-Lord, let me bless people no matter what other people have said about them. I humble myself like a child and will think like Christ Jesus concerning all people and ignore the multitudes. When Jesus got ready to heal the two blind men, he ignored the multitudes and favored the two blind men and came closer to them because they were without sight and wanted to be healed. All people need God's love even if they are not like others, we honor those who are not liked by the multitudes. Matthew 14:13-21, Mark 6:31-44, Luke 9:12-17, John 6:1-14.

-Lord, let not leaderships and people be used to hinder the love of God from others who have a physical or mental illness. Unless leaders and people humble themselves like a child they will NOT enter the kingdom of heaven. -Matthew 18:1-3, humility says do good to all and you don't have to be recognized in doing so. -Matthew 18:4

-Lord let leaders and people share your love with all lord, we humble ourselves like a child.-Matthew 18:1-4

-Lord Jesus ignore the multitudes and come closer to me so that I may see you because you love me and you favor me, despite what people have said about me, I ask to see your love for me, just like a child, I humble myself as if I were a child. -Matthew 18:1-4

-Lord, let me see that major platforms and popularity do not make prophets or leaders saved, they just make a lot of noise if their major platforms are not lived from a place of Godly love and not making money off their congregations.

-Lord let me see that followers will come and go. That relationship with you God Jesus was never really based on many followers or not. It was always based on love because you were not called to appease people who needed to hear the truth about themselves and they did not follow your ministry anymore, but Christ Jesus i'll make the right choice and I'll stay with you the one who brings in the followers and when the wrong ones leave i'll let them go, because they showed they could not handle the truth about following you Christ Jesus. If people love God Jesus, they will follow him to the cross and beyond. I will humble myself like a child God Jesus and go wherever you send me.

-Lord Jesus let no leaders make an excuse why the impoverished and sick or in their churches and congregations are leaving their churches the same way they came. Maybe teachers and leaders can ask people in their congregations who are impoverished and sick every Sunday or bible studies and leadership give their money away to them. -Matthew 18:1-4

-Lord let me see that Preaching was not meant to be from Sunday from to Sunday, but a lifestyle lived everyday ill preach to a few people who would be blessed by me than just on Sundays or bible study nights -Matthew 18:1-4

-Lord what I preach should be what I live but what I preach must not always be on the pulpit or major platform. I humble myself like a child.-matthew 18:1-4

-Lord let people humble themselves like a child and do

what people need from them to do. Lord let me ask people I don't know if they need anything. A Just because blessing to them like God loves me.

-Lord, if I have a high level of the word of God in me, let it be used to steal lost souls from satan. Lord, if I see my loved ones lost in my home, or out on the streets, or anywhere I go, let me be a blessing to them, they could be lonely, or have people in their families who are not really for them.

-Lord let leadership Not forsake the 99 but go after the one lost sheep in God's kingdom. -Matthew 18:12-14 For any leaders who have a great many people in their congregations who focus on the 99 who follow them, the 99 will always be with you but the lost ones will not. Will you go seek the lost sheep out? What about being healed from that habitual addiction of the 99 to ask God how to find the lost sheep. God is healing leaderships from habitual dark addictions that come with having that many people in their congregations.

-Lord, let there be healing for all generals, leaders, and believers who use ministry work as a habitual addiction. It's not the ministry it's the relationship with God and honor to your servants. Christ Jesus did nothing but honor those who served him, spent time with each servant, taught them, loved them, and did not ever forsake them or condemn them, if he did, he would not have had any servants. Could it be the lord is saying to his leaderships watch what you say to people who serve under you and how you treat them if leaders want their ministries healthy and strong. They would not condemn their servants or force their servants to serve them. These types of leaders need to watch how they treat those who work for them, and their servants sacrifice from their own families just to serve their leaders' ministries especially if they are not getting paid for their talents and sacrifices. Leaders should always honor those who serve them, and daily bless them. Let humble ourselves like a child and do so. Matthew 18:1-4

The word of the lord
The lord says:
How many leaderships are willing to humble themselves and wash the dishes with their servants after big dinners, clean their own churches with their servants, or reach out to their servant's families to honor them, to serve with their servants in their churches. Don't just watch in the spirit realm your servants doing your work, no, humble yourselves as a child and spend as much time with your servants as they need, they could be going through personal things, they could be sick or poor, they could need personal prayer, or counseling, or mentoring, or just guidance that need your visionary skills and love. Christ Jesus saw this in ministry with his disciples. Never overlook the needs of those who serve under you, they could be in your ministry to take your churches to its next level. They could be who God want you to pass down your ministry to. Their servants could have what their leaderships need.- Matthew 18:1-4

The word of the lord
The lord says:
-Leaderships base their main incomes, support in ministry from those who have always followed them but leaders have not sought after the lost sheep of the house. You don't have to have a physical ailment to be sick, nor anything mentally wrong or right with you. There could be Leaderships who are pride sick

because of how they are doing their ministries showing people in their congregations and the world a kingdom not of the heavenly father-1 john 2:15-17, - Matthew 4:1-12 chapter,- Luke 4:1-8 chapter. This is where leaderships needs healing from hell because of the prideful and arrogant lifestyles they show their congregations and the world. Their major platforms, titles, high positions, popularity, faithful followers, congregations' money, big houses and nice cars and won't even put impoverished people in their homes from in their churches or out on the streets, They don't give out their own pockets to impoverished people who follow them in their congregations. There are leaderships who won't give their cars away to people who do not have cars in their congregations. These leaderships who have big congregations don't even know their servants by name. These leaderships won't even work with their servants when it comes to winning lost souls. Why does winning lost souls always have to be in churches? God Jesus never did that in the way he did ministry. God Jesus told me this: "people get who and what they put first". It's what leadership and people are putting first. When God Jesus is not first in their lives from their hearts. These day's leaderships think they can use their major platforms and spread discord, but they better humble themselves like a child because the very ones they want to see in hell, God Jesus, could make those same leaders and believers be put in the same place. Matthew 18:1-4

-Lord, I pray to let what people know and have understanding be put into action, what Christ Jesus knew he acted upon. Delivered the woman caught in adultery from sexual sin, removed the judgmental pharisees out her face, and delivered her from death. Through his redemptive work with the holy father. He gave the woman caught in adultery another chance not to sin anymore, and he was merciful to her, protecting her from men who wanted to harm her. Gave the woman caught in adultery another chance at life, and love. Healed the woman caught in adultery from deception, even though she was guilty, Christ Jesus saw her innocence. He humbled himself like a child and blessed her body.-John 8:1-11

-Lord, let me be healed from the presence of deception and restore your presence to me and all the nations. Lord reveal your healing presence and bring healing from all sin in Jesus name

-Lord let people know and humble themselves that they do not need lots of money to start ministry and don't even need bank loans. Ministry starts with our relationship with Christ Jesus from your heart and you build up ministry with those around you. Relationship with Christ Jesus is what more people should depend on than their followers because they will come and go, and leaders have to accept that. Lust for big ministries should not be drawing people to their ministries. Godly love is what makes people see the change Christ Jesus does in people. Relationship with Christ Jesus is supposed to sustain people the holy way if leaderships or believer's ministries are going through difficult times. Start sincere genuine ministry in your relationship with Jesus, and he will manifest the kingdom of heaven as you follow him and keep his commandments.

-Lord like a child I humble myself to help me lord against crooked minded and crooked hearted ungodly leaders who are teachers of the gospel. Lord, I ask you to put milestones around their necks and protect me from their authority. I come to you like a child Jesus, I humble myself, lord I pray for their healing of sins that their authority won't send them to hell. Matthew 18:3 unless they repent, change, and undo their judgements. -Matthew 18:4 Because they were supposed to love all, we pass no judgements on Godly obedient repentant people of the lord.

-Lord let not leadership and generals use kingdom authority to condemn people who talk about them or their ministries, we love our enemies, and if we do condemn them, we better be the very same ones who humble ourselves and seek to save them if they humble themselves and repent.

-Lord again heal the use of authority in your kingdom, we humble ourselves like a child, we depend on your authority lord Jesus to prevail over the authority of ungodly leaders and teachers of the gospel of faith. Lord Jesus, you love me, I ask for love.

-Lord let my labor for you be protected and my oil healed by your holy presence to cover my labor in your kingdom because I serve you uprightly. -Psalm 84:11 you will not withhold anything from them who are upright. - Psalm 145:8-9 you love me lord, lord you are good to all, compassionate to all, lord do good to me because you have the power to. Lord heal all nations from hell, you delight not in the death of anybody. -Ezekiel 18:32

-Lord, I pray that you do good because you have the power to. matthew 18:1-4

-Lord let me daily give you fresh a yes lord every day, it's just what I love to do, i'll brush my teeth and use mouthwash daily just to bring my mouth under your authority lord in jesus name

-Lord, heal and protect my thoughts from hell, don't let my thoughts put me in a place like that. you lord will change the way I think about you showing me if you are willing, lord let condemning thoughts be broken off in jesus name.

-Lord all things are possible with God. -Matthew 19:26

-Lord, let me practice your prayers, and not just my prayers. Lord Jesus I honor you what are your prayers I can live and practice this day, because you love me Jesus.

-Lord Jesus you keep doing all things, do all things lord I prophesy to you

-Lord you will do anything for me, because you love me, I honor you. -Matthew 18:1-4

-Lord remove from my life anything or anyone who wants to take your place as first, lord let me not live in the sinful flesh, lord let me not be seduced by false prophecies that I put them first, love does not seek its own – 1 Corinthians 13:5 i no longer have to live underneath the law of sin and death because there is grace in christ jesus, and not just through ministry of unholy leaders..

-Lord we the nations can't take any more of your beatings let us heal from them because you love us, but like a child you love us and watch over us love us despite our consequences lord we humble ourselves like a child and don't hold it against you holy father. Lord heal all the nations from your beatings, lord you're stronger than us in eternity and we must fear you. There must be change with repentance. Lord drive out sin in all our inner spirits. Set our inner spirits free. in jesus name

-Lord, let me honor God and honor people.

-Lord let us keep loving lost souls like it's the last day to live and repent..

-Lord, your word says in 1 John 1:7-9 you will cleanse us from all unrighteousness. Lord leaders and believers must decide to stay clean and live clean before you, we can't live in the sin of unclean relationships and expect for you to cleanse us to keep sinning that's not a real surrender. We must let go of unclean relationships if not Galatians 5:19-21 says no unclean people go to heaven and no adultery enters into the kingdom of heaven unless they repent and let Jesus change them with judgements. We must decide to live before our lord clean or not because unclean relationships separate us from you God. If unclean relationships are put first than you lord, then people in unclean lifestyles are without you. God the father you are NOT an unclean God, you don't give us what's unclean to people and God Jesus you did ministry a divine clean spirit.

-Lord let lost souls be won first in our lives rather than before the riches of the world.

-Lord let us as believers watch what doctrines we eat from in churches, leaders could be preaching to steal people's heavenly names and heavenly identities preaching to people who don't know who they are to God the father concerning their heavenly names and heavenly identities because of lack of knowledge, lack of studying, and what's hidden in the heart of leaderships from the deception of riches.- Mark 4:19

-Lord let all the tormented people be healed of all their afflictions. -Mark 5:34

-Lord no longer afflict your people where you have afflicted them. Nahum 1:9-12

-Lord let us humble ourselves and help struggling people. If God shows us that, we won't put burdens on others that they cannot carry, we would bear their burdens.

-Lord let leaders and people keep loving lost souls until they decide to have a saving relationship with the lord.

-Lord, let leaders, generals and believers give up their selfish desires. -2 Timothy 3:1-2 says men will become lovers of themselves. Matthew 18:3 Unless they humble themselves like a child they will not go to heaven.

-Lord let leaders and believers be accountable for lost souls they could have used the word of God to save them. And lord you would have been faithful to that word, let leaders intercede for all people with love.

-lord yet again and again and again heals the nations from

hell, lord let us stop sinning against you, let the nations stop sinning and heal them if they want healing and want to continue in a relationship with you.

-Lord let us together reject leaders who preach leaven bread and the false prophetic opinions and motives of their hearts and minds. -Matthew 18:1-4

-Lord i pray that God's people not put first the sin of their leaders

-Lord heal me from all evil and protect my soul- psalm 121:7-8

-Lord, I can't do this by myself. I need for you to fight for me, Isaiah 41:10 I ask for love where I have been influenced with evil because of the end times.

-Lord let leaders and believers pray for people having a positive mindset for them, let me have their best interest at mind and heart, and when you show me things you have for them, I will NOT hold them back from God's love or his blessings.

-Lord let not leadership and believers have a positive mindset about others who are not like them, lord help disabled people who are being misjudged by doctors, their families, and people around them because they don't have knowledge like others, maybe leaders and people could invest in them knowledge and blessings.

-Lord, let me humble myself as a child and want the best for all people whether I'm in their life or not. I will humble myself like a child and still love them -Matthew 18:1-4.

-Lord let me humble myself like a child and want to see my enemies be healed from their sins and restored if they repent and I do not have to know them well or not, I put my faith in the love God has for them. Christ Jesus died for sins over 2,000 years ago.

-Christ Jesus said love your enemies -Matthew 5:44

-Lord you said a man's enemies will be those in their house-holds.-Matthew 10:36

-Lord let me humble myself like a child and not be afraid to show my enemies kindness or favor, something I practiced and lived and did in street ministry and something I practice and live by in my home.

–Lord, let me humble myself like a child and offer my forgiveness to my enemies and friends if I know them well or not. Because if I forgive them from my heart I would not keep bringing up what they did I would keep going as if it never happened.

-Lord let me humble myself like a child and practice praying for others more than I do myself, lord let me pray for my enemies, let me pray for my friends, and even relatives. I want the best for them because you love them.

-Lord let me humble myself like a child and not ever be too busy working my own dreams that I won't call a love one and check on them, no, show me the errors lord of my shortcomings to see how they are doing or go out my way to be a blessing to people around me just because I should not forsake to bless people when it comes to me working my own ambitions and aspirations.

-Be a blessing to people just because to make a difference In people's lives, if your at the store, restaurant, or gas station, or wherever are maybe do a just because blessing for people around you, why would people accumulate wealth from the world and not be a blessing to others around them, God show me in me in the spirit and let me locate the impoverished ones that are sleeping In the cold out on the streets and they are homeless and have no home or heat to keep them warm, they could be sick, lord open my eyes to this and let me locate them, and be a blessing to them serve them.

-Lord let leaders and believers humble themselves like a

child and share all their knowledge with people, just because leaders, doctors, and Politicians have more knowledge than others they can tell others the Godly truth and do not hold God's people back from knowledge because doctors know more than them. Lord let leaders and believers be judged for holding back knowledge from people they look down upon in their hearts or what other people have said about them. Matthew 18:1-4.

-Lord let people humble themselves and let sinful pride be cast out of minds and heart's exchange for love in people's minds and thoughts if they would love others with upright minds and won't hide things in their minds from others. -Matthew 18:1-4

-Lord let leaders and believers humble themselves not to take advantage of others in their minds, let the wicked forsake their thoughts -Isaiah 55:7 lord let them humble themselves and be renewed in the spirit of their minds. -Ephesians 4:22-24.

-Lord let leaders and believers humble themselves and love the lost people more than what they do themselves, that more leaders and believers will continually seek for them to have the love of God until its their last day to live, that's how important lost souls are to God. That's how much leaderships and believers would want to keep offering lost people the love of God, only God knows people's hearts, not people, who are leaders and believers to hinder the love of God from lost people, no, let leaderships and believers humble themselves and offer the love of God to all people, so that they will No longer be lost. More people should be doing more to win lost souls for God. There is absolutely no excuse why leadership and believers are not going after lost souls.

-Lord let me humble myself like a child let me be sent to people where I can meet them right where they are in their hearts whatever place they may be in. lord let me be willing to share God's blessings with my enemies and people. Sharing God's blessings of healing with enemies in my home and in my family.

From working my faith and love from a place of Christ Jesus cross to believe for people to be saved right where they are. In my greeting love card ministry on the streets I enjoyed sharing God's blessings with people who really could have been my enemies in their hearts, it's what I loved to do and now I write this book of upright pocket prayers to keep my promise to God Jesus to honor his heart and to honor God the father and honor people with humble prayers that God Jesus taught me to live before him so people can share with others what God has so richly blessed me with for others. So, people can learn to practice living humble prayers to please God. It's always how people live from the heart. and mind before God and not about the way people preach. God the Father sees all people through Christ Jesus' blood of atonement over 2,000 years ago if only people will repent and obey Christ Jesus by reading about him. So, instead of people only saying prayer with only their lips, they can live by humble prayers of action through the righteousness of Christ Jesus blood of atonement because we are made righteous by his blood of atonement and not through our own works that's God Jesus, relationship works are under Gace.

-Lord your sovereign, let it never be too late for those people who serve Christ Jesus and obey him because he loves people and does not want to see them lost and without him. Christ Jesus' heart doesn't want that for people. Christ Jesus did good at the last minute until death in the presence of his enemies. Christ Jesus died for people's sins, people are justified through Christ Jesus blood of atonement, we are sanctified through the blood of Christ Jesus he was rejected on the cross because he loved until death and beyond the crossover 2,000 years ago.

-Lord let me be sanctified from rejection through Christ Jesus' cross over 2,000 years ago.

-Lord I am not called unto impurity but the sanctification of the lord. -1 Thessalonians 4:7

-Lord let people humble themselves like a child, let them be healed, lord heal all from the curse, corruption, and condemnation by us staying with Christ Jesus, through the blood of Christ Jesus.

-Lord, let your sons who abuse their authority and lead in your kingdom be stricken with a rod to deliver them from hell. -proverbs 23:14

-Lord no longer let leaders show a kingdom to the world without you holy father.

-Lord I let your love change my heart and mind.

-Lord let people be teachable, you will teach the humble your way for those who humble themselves.

-Lord, when the humble are teachable they do not have to concern themselves with living a prideful and arrogant life.

-Lord let our minds and hearts be healed of its sins, don't let leaders and believers be a friend in their hearts but an enemy in their minds when it comes to serving you, let us be humble in mind and hearts. Sin shall not have dominion over us in those places because of the end times.

-Lord let all hearts and minds be restored, I speak Jesus over every heart and mind, lord daily restore our souls, and heal all from hell if people repent through the redemptive work of Christ Jesus.

-Lord let my private living of the heart and mind align with my public living of the heart and mind, lord – I humble myself like a child lord daily cleanse our hearts and minds from where sin seeks to reside. The blood of Jesus breaks sin and iniquity in the hearts and minds of people if they apply the blood of Christ Jesus

-Lord let our minds and hearts be childlike just like Christ Jesus, give us the integrity to face ourselves. Lord people need to humble themselves; lord keep our spirits checked and corrected by daily reading the word of God.

-Lord let us do what Christ Jesus needs us to do, we are his answered prayer, and NOT his hindrance in the things he tells us to do, or places he sends us, if leadership and believers will humble themselves like a child.

-Lord let us all be healed from the afflictions of our minds - Mark 5:34, lord heal our minds from what the enemy started for evil, lord heal all our minds from hell, lord I pray for the healing of all the nations concerning hearts and minds, lord I pray remove from us any evil, or sin in our hearts and minds because you want us to get right with you in those places, let us all repent.

-Lord, take away evil from all disabled people. We speak together. They are healed, they all walk, let all their eyes be opened, they that hath an ear let them hear, demons let their all minds and bodies be loosed, and let all disabled people be healed and loved. People should NOT treat them differently because of their true conditions, or judge them from what people say about them, lord let leadership and believers be a blessing to all disabled people.

CHAPTER 10

Word of love to the healing of all the nations

I just wanted to share my Godly knowledge and wisdom of childlike faith so God's people and generals would NOT go to hell from pride and arrogance and lose their souls because they serve their own lust in ministry having dark and hidden addictions. God hates pride and arrogance. So, I put together these prayers in this book to bless anyone who wants change. I'm not hurting anyone in this prayer book, I'm blessing anyone and to share his heart to keep my promise to Christ Jesus and what I prophesied to him at my rose bush at home. Proverbs 18:16-17 says a man's gift maketh room for them, and bringeth them before great men. God Jesus gave me gifts of healing and miracles for his people, the gift of creativity biblically and creative prayers for people to intercede for people who do not know how to be creative in. Godly wisdom, church goers who do not get creativity from their pastors and leaderships concerning healing. I have the gift of rapture because

my name is rainbow, the gift of the sun because the rainbow is the sun, the gift of multicolored wisdom and other gifts he gave me great things I'm tapping into. God Jesus cultivates them, so I no longer focus on jobs that do not cultivate my gifts because of the money they offer. When God gives people a vision of their gifts, we are going to have to give up jobs that are a hindrance to your gifts and having life in Christ Jesus his way. God Jesus is teaching me to share my gifts he gave me with others the anointing and mantles over my life. That if people want what I got from me they would humble themselves like a child and ask me for an impartation so they would not be jealous in their hearts. Like God Jesus did with his disciples, the Pharisees were jealous because they did not humble themselves and ask Jesus when he prompted them to ask. Asking for something you want from others is wisdom instead of not wanting people to have what they labored for. -1 John 5:14 says that if people ask anything according to his will, he will give to them, -Matthew 7:7-8 says ask and it shall be given seek and ye shall find.

Lord I pray let not disabled people be taken advantage of because many of them do not have the knowledge like others and they do not know how to pray for themselves let leaders give them honest knowledge where they suffer mentally and pray for them according to have God's best interest for them at heart from God's heart.

-lord, let not leadership and believers ever take advantage of people who do not know how to pray themselves, if they do, lord judge them in anger righteously and visit their iniquity. -Numbers 14:18.

-Lord let all the tormented disabled people be healed from hell and all false identities be broken off their lives and forgive them lord Jesus, they don't know how to pray for themselves, but you lord the son of man hath power to forgive sins. Mark 2:10.

-Lord let us all obey our bibles; lord I pray we must seek you; lord heal the nations that seek you and obey you.

-Lord, let me minister to the ones who salted my name.

-Lord let me walk the narrow path that I may find in life, The Broadway leadeth many people to destruction. -Matthew 7:13-14, lord Jesus there is no other way of living than your divine way of living through you the holy way, your way Christ Jesus and not through the law of sin and death, as it says in Romans 8 chapter.

-Lord let there be healing for your generals, leaders, and believers from the lust of ministry, followers will not be their lust and their money, their big churches will not be my lust, their titles, high position in the temples, and popularity will not be their lust, nor their authority will not be their lust. Romans 6:23 says for the wages of sin is death but the gift of God eternal life. James 1:15 says when lust is conceived it brings death.

-Lord give life to your leaderships and people where death is meant, lord heal the nations from the consequences of hell, lord let there be change in hearts and minds.

-Lord I'm willing to give up my big churches' buildings, my title, my major platform, my high positions in order to show the world a kingdom from you holy father. If I have to go down to 12 people, it will be the people who I protect to go to the next levels in my relationship with you. - 1 john 2:16-17

-Lord let me serve you with a right heart and right mind, lord create in me a clean heart and renew a right spirit within me, psalm 51:10-12 lord I pray heal all hearts where they were hardened because of sin, lord healing for the nations, lord more healing for our sins against you. lord be merciful and heal souls for your people have sinned against you psalm 41.

-Lord let all leaders and believers be honest and not be liars -psalm 120:2 says you will deliver and heal them from lying lips and from a deceitful tongue, lord let leaders and believers be truthful and honest with all.

-Lord let all nations change the way they think, healing for the nations, lord heal all thoughts of the mind, lord let all thoughts be pure. Lord break yokes off our thoughts Matthew 5:8 The pure in heart shall see God, we are forgiven if we repent through Christ Jesus' blood over 2,000 years ago because the power of sin is too strong for us, lord let us repent of sin.

-Lord let us all choose to forgive from our hearts, thus I ask you to remove offence from our hearts that we all may have the grace to forgive others, because Christ Jesus forgave us - Ephesians 4:32.

-Lord let me help people as much as they ask, just like you're always helping me when I pray or ask for you. Lord has been my eternal help.

-Lord Let me humble myself like a child.

-Lord let me humble myself greater than children.

-Humility comes before honor lord let me humble myself

-Lord teach me the ways of the humble, I'm teachable

-lord your grace is with the humble, I practice humbling myself.

-Lord, your word says you resist the proud and give grace to the humble-James 4:6-7.

-Proverbs 16:18 says pride goes before destruction, and a haughty spirit before a fall.

-Lord I pray your word says humble yourselves before the lord and he will lift you up, God pour out grace to those who practice humility.

-Lord let our minds and hearts be innocent like a child humble, dependent, trusting and weak lord grant eternal daily healing for how we serve you.

-Lord let me give up anything or anyone to follow you

-Lord let me give up materialistic things that hinder me from walking in humility and not humbling myself.

-Lord let me see the needs of those around me, and be a blessing to them.

-Lord I pray I humble myself like a child until I can't just for you to get the glory and the honor be put on only you lord, I'm not concerned with having my own honor, for you lord are to be honored in all things before myself, I will not steal your glory lord for all things are underneath your control and authority.

-Lord, send me to those people who are lost in my family. I humble myself, what is on your heart for them, how can I win their souls for you to bring you glory.

-Lord, I humbled myself as a child and I go visit the sick, I clothe the naked, and visit those who were in prison, feed those who were hungry.

-Lord I pray as leaderships and believers that we humble ourselves from your wounds, lord heal my wounds if thou hast afflicted me, it was for my good that I learn not to sin, as long as you still love me, i'll stay with you even though you did not want the consequences for me, lord thank you for loving me and teaching me, because like a child I fear your authority. Nahum 1:9-12 lord where you afflicted us you will afflict no longer for you changed your mind.

-Lord, I pray you if I take my words back, you will take your words back. You have changed your mind. -Jeremiah 15:19-21

-Lord let me love those who have a love problem; however they may challenge me to love them, I will love them anyway even if I have to distance myself for a while away from them I'll keep going back to them because they are loved by Christ Jesus.

-Lord the gospel tells me there is nothing new under the Sun in Ecclesiastes, but you changed your mind and in Isaiah 43: 18-19 to do a new thing.

-Lord let there be an outpouring for more healing for the nations from hell, lord save all the nations like it's they last day to live if they repent

-Lord let me listen to hurting people cry out to you, and how can I bless them with your heart for them God to heal them and be a blessing to them. Lord, how can I bless the hurting with grace today? How shall I humble myself and serve you Jesus today?

-Lord I pray to do for me what I do for others, acknowledge my relationship with you against my enemies, for you will favor me like the two blind men.

-Lord let grace heal the hurting of their sins lord heal the hurting from hell lord, lord save all their lost souls, and bring them closer to you, heal their relationship with you, and restore them where sin separated them from you.

-Lord give Grace to the separated to be restored back to you if there is repentance.

-Lord, I pray to break demons off all the nations of people's lives, lord break demons that want to destroy the nations, the anointing destroys all yokes, lord break demons off the nations and let them go free.

-Lord let hell lose another soul and they are free.

-Lord let me have freedom in the spirit, where the spirit of the lord is there is liberty

-Lord believers should humble themselves to be corrected by the word of God in their relationship with lord.

-Lord if leaders have had a relationship with you longer

than others, they can still be corrected by you even though they teach the gospel, I will as a teacher of gospel I will not use a major platform to not be teachable or corrected by you lord.

-Lord as leaders or teachers of the gospel correction purges me if I obey it wholeheartedly to increase in your holy presence, and demons know me by what I let go and sacrifice for you and to sacrifice what never showed the world love and Jesus that was your way.

-Lord let I pray send me to those who are deemed lesser than authority than me and I'll serve you from that place in your heart.

-Lord i'll humble myself so much that i'll bless people in secret just between me and you and I do not have to get recognized by it, ill humble myself like a child to please you only between me and you.

-Lord I pray they do not have to remember me but they remember you Lord in my relationship with you, lord as long as you remember me on that day I stand before your heavenly kingdom in eternity and you will judge lord my work on the earth.

-Lord, I'll sacrifice my major platform just to honor you and show the world Jesus in other places than just my churches.

-Lord let me give up my popularity as I live the gospel.

-Lord if I have a high position in the temples and churches bring me to my lowest estate because your mercy endures forever -psalm 136:23

-Psalm 86:13 says lord great is your love that you deliver people from the lowest hell, lord deliver me for I do not want to be without you.

-Lord I pray how great is your mercy, that you should save my soul

-Lord, I pray to remove every hindrance in our inner spirits that will put us in that place. in jesus name

-Lord I pray deliver the all the nations from their place in hell in jesus name

-Lord, I pray for greater healing from hell in the nations, until they all are healed, and changed if they want healing for their sins.

-Lord if leaders, teachers, or prophets have a title in these churches let me be silent about it and win souls closer to you without them even knowing who I am, who I am is for your glory lord.

-Lord, I pray in ministry or in a relationship with God. It's not about my name, for my ministry is not supposed to be named after myself, but the ruler of the earth.

-Lord, if I'm a teacher of the gospel or leader, send me to places where I can be a light for your glory.

-Lord let me show the world Jesus loves your way and not the pride of life. -matthew 4:1-12

-Lord your word says in proverbs those who despise correction shall die, but the wise can be corrected.-proverbs 15:3

-Lord let believers bow the sins of their minds underneath your feet and authority. Lord save all the nations who have left you because they gave up on you, bring the prodigals home, heal apostasy lord I pray the nations need healing.

-Lord let there be an outpouring of healing from you spirit in the seasons to come and in these end times, lord all the nations need you, lord hear the all the cries of the nations.

-Lord heal all minds and thoughts of the nations, lord save all the nations from the way they think.

-Lord let me love beyond myself, it's more to life than just me and myself, help me share the love of god your way, help me love beyond myself lord in what you have given me, cause me to sacrifice and give up things that other people need more than me, if it's my cars I never drive, a bed I have that I never sleep in, or money I don't spend, or clothes I do not wear, someone said this that selfish teachers and believers lose more than what they started with and that's their souls.

-Lord, I pray that you will convict your generals who have major platforms to heal like Christ Jesus healed in their churches.

-What profits men to gain the whole world and lose their souls. -mark 8:34-38

-Lord let not selfish leaders lose their souls, major platforms have done that to them, their selfish desires and selfish gain in their hearts. Major platforms will not be dark addictions that they show their congregations.

-Lord let not leadership deceive their congregations by showing them a kingdom not of the father, lord let not leadership be without the father in ministry.

-Lord I pray let not your generals be without the heavenly father because of them showing a kingdom not of the father , lord heal them from pride and arrogance, heal them from addictions that come with ministry, lord save your generals from that stench of pride, and you told them to pass down their ministries, but the churches were too big filled with congregation money, what they hide in their hearts let their members see.

-Lord heal your generals from dark addictions in ministry, lord heal them in that area and save their souls from hell because major platforms are their lust, lord let the lost sheep mean more to them than the 99 who will always be there.-let not mass ministries lay in the nuptial bed. psalm 139, places of unfulfillment of ministry.

-Lord let there not be premature death in leaderships from lust, pride, and arrogance.

-Lord let there not be anything hidden in their hearts they do not tell others concerning the sin of lust of leaders, prophets, and teachers of the gospel. Even on popular christian networks places of unfulfillment.

-Lord help your leaders see they do not have to do ministry always with major platforms, more healing lord from major platforms for your leaders.

-Lord let the nations pray for leaders who all need healing from hell from being without their heavenly father. Though both Jesus and the father hang out with many lost people they did in the gospels, God's generals and leadership are still loved even though the pride of life makes them lost. Matthew 4:1-12, Luke 4:1-12.

-Lord, I pray let not lust be the cause of death in churches from leadership lord, give them all life and heal them from hell lord, save them lord, and show them what the kingdom of heaven looks like without major platforms and popularity of the gospel.

-Lord, I pray god's generals and leadership will NOT die the death of lust and the pride of life, and lose their souls, even though they have been preaching the gospel longer than others, their major platforms look good to their congregations, but major platforms are making leaderships lost.

-Lord, I pray to heal your leaders from the trap of the pride of life, lord heal them all from the curse of pride and arrogance, lord redeem the lives of your servants. -psalm 34:22.

-So, I hear the lord say leeches the leaderships leech spirit in churches, churches being a place of unfulfillment people who are leaving churches the same way they came in, leaving sick in their bodies, there pastors sucking financially from their congregations, the leech spirit does not fulfill its just takes and takes and takes.

-Lord let leaders not financially be stuck from their congregations to enrich themselves.

-Lord, I pray that leaders do not focus on taking financial

money from their congregations and they have not healed sick bodies in their congregations like Christ Jesus did.

-Let Christ Jesus not be sad- rivers of living water Jesus give your leaderships drink and generals drink they have been thriving off congregations and leaderships are not fulfillment with the 99, lord give them drink for their ministry addictions heal them all from hell so you will not be sad Jesus, save your generals and leaderships lord let there be an outpouring of healing in the nations.

-Lord, I pray let not ministry be their sin, for they are without you but lord Jesus you hang around lost people everyday you did it in the gospel all the time, for the son man came to save those who are lost.

-Lord let your leadership humble themselves and be there for people who need them the most but personally with each servant who does serve them, and church's members who attend their churches.

-Lord, I pray I will sacrifice my selfish desires because there is no selfish gain in myself. Lord give me a heart that would benefit others of the love of God to those who need to see me without any selfish desires.

-Lord, I pray that you help me see what I have to give up and sacrifice so that it will no longer be a hindrance , even if it's people or materialistic things

-Lord, I pray that you remove those who have major platforms who do not walk in love, lord take their major platforms away from them, because they left the wilderness without you but took what the wilderness offered without you. Lord, I pray to heal them all from pride and arrogance lord save their souls.

-Lord Jesus, you redeem anything and anyone- the oil of redemption for the healing of the nations.

-Lord turns the wicked people into winning warriors, Jesus

changes everything. Mark 2:18-22. Jesus changes anyone. -2 Corinthians 5:17

-Lord turn the evil people into empowering and elevating epistles of the gospel of faith, Jesus changes everything mark 2:18-22, Jesus changes anyone. -2 Corinthians 5:17

-Lord let me live in humility that brings wisdom- proverbs 11:2

-Lord, I ask for the anointing of humility that breaks the yoke of pride and arrogance. Let me be willing to give up anything that makes me prideful or arrogant.

-Humility is the fear of the lord-proverbs 22:4

-Lord let all the humble become teachable

-Lord let me humble myself because I fear your authority

-Lord, I pray you hate pride and arrogance, so shall I.

-Lord let all people hate their vain thoughts but thy law makes them to love and put first and make priority.

-Lord, I pray that people are determined not to sin in their minds and hearts.

-Lord let there be a transformation in every heart and every mind sets of thoughts, lord heal all the nations thoughts daily- Luke 6:19

-Lord, I pray let us not do any sinning in our thoughts, let the wicked forsake their thoughts. -Isaiah 55:7

-Lord let us return to you, and you will have mercy: and to our god, for he will abundantly pardon. -Isaiah 55:7

- Jesus healed them all, and he will heal me- Luke 6:19

-Lord I pray send your word and heal the nations from their destruction

-Lord let me live your ways of humility through my heart and mind

-Lord, I ask you to teach me humility and remove any pride and arrogance from me, lord I humble myself like a child.

-Lord, I pray let all people love you with all their hearts, souls, and minds and strength. -Matthew 22:37-40

-Lord help me to humble myself greater than a child. Lord let me not be childish but child-like -Matthew 18:4

-The beginning fear of the lord is to hate evil; God hates evil behaviors, God hates arrogant pride, and hates every wicked way, and a mouth of perversion. God hates perversion -proverbs 8:13

-Lord delight in me as I surrender any pride or arrogance. Lord, I pray I keep humbling myself like a child.

-Lord, I pray to give your generals and leadership humble hearts and humble minds for the saving of their souls and heal them from any evil behaviors or sinful way.

-Lord I pray healing oil again over evil minds and evil hearts, lord make evil hearts and minds good hearts and good minds, lord heal evil, lord Jesus your love conquers evil.

-Lord let not people throw their enemies away, let them humble themselves like a child and pray healing oil over their enemies' minds and hearts. They could have no one praying for them. We should not be afraid to show our enemy's favor whether we agree with their ways or not, Christ Jesus died for all over 2,000 years ago.

-Lord make my humble Godly sacrifices come from the redemptive work of your cross over 2,000 years, that's how I drink your blood and eat your body. -John 6:54

CHAPTER 11
Just because blessings

ord you will consider our lowest state your mercy endures for ever-psalm 136:23-26. Healing for all the nations from hell through love

-The lord will rescue the nations from their enemies for his mercy endures forever. -psalm 136:23-26

-God gives food to all his mercy endures forever. -psalm 136:23-26

-God satisfies the desire of the afflicted people. -Isaiah 58:10

-Lord, heal all lives from evil or sin if people will humble themselves and repent, lord as I stay repentant to find grace, let me seek you lord and keep you first.

-Lord, for your generals and leadership's ministry work should not always come first before the well- being of their servants, that's selfish pride of them. Lord, I pray to let them humble themselves like a child. do they personally spend time with their workers who serve them or is their churches too big for them to do that. Or do they want their servants to do all the work, Jesus taught his servants teamwork he spent personal time with each of his disciples.

-Lord let people never forsake a lost soul around them to get recognized by the rich, let us do the work around us of doing something to bring a lost soul closer to Christ Jesus love.

-Lord, I pray that you will deliver me from my transgressions.

-Heavens oil in all things. Mark 6:13 And they cast out demons and anointed with oil many who were sick and healed them.

Heaven's oil heals all things. -Matthew 19:26 says all things are possible with God.

-Lord let me have a creative healing and peace- john 14:23

-Lord, I pray daily and direct all my thoughts to stay focused on God's love, I humble myself like a child.

-Lord I pray do new miracles because of your love for me

-Lord let there be new miracles in my mind, heart, and thoughts

-Lord let there be new miracles for the nations

-Lord you did not give me a spirit of fear, but of love power and of a sound mind.

-Lord, I ask for a sound mind that drives out fear.

-Lord I ask for a sound mind that drives any evil, perfect those things that concern me, lord I pray.

-Lord let me have a sound mind that pleases you, you see my mind and heart through christ jesus blood over 2,000 years ago, his redemptive work

-Lord let the nation's mindsets stay underneath your authority, leaders should not use their minds to be servants of unrighteousness.

Lord let all the nations bow their hearts and minds at christ jesus feet of love and mercy

-Lord I bow my lips unto your blood of atonement over 2,000 years, my mind and heart should be used for your glory, lord Jesus apply your blood of atonement on my lips and thoughts forever

-Lord I pray do not let sin have dominion over me, set me free through Christ jesus redemptive work over 2,000 years ago.

-Lord let me stay repentant in mercy concerning mind, thoughts and heart sins.

-Lord I pray let the blood of Christ Jesus break sins, and break sin off lives and souls.

-Lord let there be a daily cleansing in my mind, thoughts, and heart, just for you to keep my sins forgiven.

-Lord, cause me to be continually cleansed to be cleansed not unto unclean relationships, but cleansed that I make stay right with you under grace.

-Lord, I pray let the nations be healed from sin.

-Lord I daily repent you daily restore me because of your blood Lord jesus

-Lord I pray daily to restore my mind and heart, renew me from sin, because I should not put it first, I need you to change me from my sins, lord Jesus nothing stays the same with you.

-Lord I pray let the nations watch who they put first, their leaders and teachers could be self-enriched from their congregations, lord let us be more aware of who we put first and who we follow.

-Lord I pray let people humble themselves like a child and do really sweet things for people they know nothing about on their jobs, in stores, in homes, in schools, riding around in new cars, for street walkers, and they did not even have to ask you, it was done from a place people already have and that's from the heart.

-Lord, I pray let there will be healing through redemption. Jeremiah 17:14 says redeem the nations lord and the nations shall be redeemed, save the nations and they shall be saved, for the nations to give you glory and honor.

-Lord, I pray that I do not forsake 1 lost soul around me to get recognized by the rich.

-Lord, show me in the spirit those who have chains on them, and let leaders, generals, and teachers humble themselves like a child and do something about it.

-Lord let me humble myself that says ill do something about people who need to see God Jesus love. Lord let people not overlook others and not pray for them, not overlooking people's true condition to get recognized by the rich. When we see lost souls on the streets, we can stop driving to go out our way to just pray for a soul and a blessing too them. Take a little time to see if they need anything you already have. Do not overlook them if you see them in the spirit realm around you praying for them, they could not have anybody praying for them the way God has given knowledge to his people.

-Lord, if leaders and believers have the power to do good, let them do good to people.

-Lord, cause me to think how I should live before you in humility. Matthew 18:1-4

-Lord, I pray that I do good to people despite what they think about me or what they say about me.-Matthew 18:1-4

-Lord show me how to love people despite what they look like.- matthew 18:1-4

-Lord, help me love people despite the fact that if they dont love themselves, give me the wisdom to minister to them, so they can feel the love of Jesus, jesus love changes lives, minds, and hearts.-matthew 18:1-4

-Lord, I pray you will teach me to think about people like you do, but how much more should we think about love for our enemies or servants. Matthew 18:1-4

-Lord, let me do what I don't understand when it comes to

having a childlike faith relationship with only jesus.- Matthew 18:1-4

-Lord let people humble themselves greater than children, the more humbling of themselves, is abounding in all grace.- matthew 18:1-4

-Lord, teach me how to think about Jesus' love for people and bless them from that place of your hearts and minds. - matthew 18:1-4

-Lord, I pray you will teach me how to help people because we would want to love them with our hearts and minds. matthew 18:1-4

-Lord, let me practice forgiving people like a child does, quickly letting go as if the offense never happened by grace and going back to what I was doing in my day. Matthew 18:1-4.

-Lord, let me bless people around me not expecting anything in return just to do good to people like Jesus would to make a difference in their lives. matthew 18:1-4

-Lord i pray let me love people like its they last day to live.- matthew 18:1-4

-Lord let people be drawn to ministries that walk in a holy love, and not just by church's names and titles.-matthew 18:1-4

-Lord let leaders, teachers, and prophets take up the sacrifice of walking in love to all people to serve without greed in their hearts.-matthew 18:1-4

-Lord let leaders, generals, and prophets heal people's lives because you see their true condition, healing people's lives is not about the money they get in churches or other buildings. Christ Jesus' manifestation of healing came because he was willing to sacrifice things he never needed in ministry. Matthew 18:1-4

-Lord let leaders, generals, and prophets do ministry like a child's heart, it's not about just working the works in ministry it is about what comes from people's hearts and minds. That's childlike faith. Giving christ jesus all of what's in hearts and minds, not by having a longer term of relationship with him. Matthew 18:1-4.

-Lord, I pray that you give leaders,generals, and prophets childlike faith hearts because we only want him first. we only honor christ jesus as first. Matthew 18:1-4

-Lord let prophets, teachers, and generals think love like children do, and they all will be greater than children in humility because leaders put away the childish things of ministry that children do not, for childlike faith hearts and minds.

-Lord, I pray that your people do not know you through perversion relationships, there is a thing called holiness, and christ jesus did not have perverse power, christ jesus did not call a female body a boy or man, he said stay inside my laws of creation one male and female.

-Lord, I pray let leaders, prophets, generals, teachers of the gospel love unselfishly, because their selfish desires are tearing God's people's lives, and more Godly men and Godly women need to stand against the sin of perversion and jezebel teachers who do have false prophecies.

-For the lord would want his men and women to get the childlike faith, we would want them to apply what we know.

-Lord let not leaders, prophets, ad generals, teachers and believers not put a price on an enemy's soul, we would want to see our enemies saved., we would not trade their souls for money nor their hearts.

-Lord let not people forsake an enemy to get recognized by the rich people.

-Lord let me forsake rich people to catch a enemy in the spirit realm

-Lord let me forsake rich people if they can't give up their riches to follow you.

-Lord let leaders, prophets, generals and believers not forsake their families to serve their relatives' enemies.

-Lord let more generals and preachers practice more healing lives like Jesus did in ministry for their congregations, and ministries. or even street healings, or hospital visit healings, or prison healings, or healing in their homes.

CHAPTER 12
My final prayer

Matthew 18:1-3 jesus said those who dont humble themselves like a child will not go to heaven but hell, christ jesus curse on his apostles he removed it through humility if they humbled themselves like a child, Matthew 18:4 jesus said those who humble themselves like a child go to heaven Jesus changed his mind and his word based off people's choices to learn humility faith and love.

-More leaders should be loving lost people around them more than what they love themselves. If you can have faith for them, God will trust you not to get recognized by the rich people or to serve him, for selfish gain in ministry. Ministry will always begin through a relationship with the lord, not always starting with people through people. i strongly believe if we put the needs of others first in the way we use kingdom authority, then we wont show the world such a selfish prideful and arrogant gospel and peoples bodies are not getting healed less their minds and hearts.

Isaiah 25:8
The lord will daily take away hell from his all his people, wipe their tears and show them all mercy

Conclusion:

I have humbled myself greater than children to honor the lord jesus to please my lord and i kept my promise to him to revise his book for souls he wants to make beautiful for jesus apostle men and bishop men and women who wanna humble themselves like a little child so people can know his heart than just his name, my promise kept to jesus and fulfilled by me Rainbow from my talk with the lord at my mom's rose bush i made a promise to him that people will bow to Christ jesus heart, and know his heart more, than what they teach in their ministries.

Live by as much faith for your enemies as leaders do for their servants.
I have humbled myself like a child to honor my enemies and celebrate each life by offering humility to people so they won't go to hell for pride and arrogance
I have honored God the father. I kept my promise to his son Jesus, we honor the God who brought forth his son christ jesus over 2,000 years ago.

-I have honored all people I don't know in this book and I celebrate and honor all lives in Jesus' book for his generals and bishop leaders, men and women. I honor all people. I honor those who are not really for me in their hearts. People buy this book of humility and wisdom, and I've ministered to those who salted my name. I have humbled myself greater than a child having faith for people I don't know, or who don't know me. Honoring the lord for teaching me childlike faith. I honor the lord again in this book for his divine glory and to his divine honor.

-I have honored my mother for placing me around children to learn the childlike faith 15 years ago, honored my family, and honored the All the Gods of heaven. I honor them by humbling myself like a child for his people.

-Jesus told me to redo, revise, and reconstruct his book, and I humbled myself like a child and obeyed him, and redid his book for all his men, or any women struggling with pride and arrogance in ministry.

-Honoring all the children lives at my moms former daycare that helped me see the world through their eyes and faith in people..

For by faith and love to jesus

- I believed in the righteousness of Christ Jesus' cross that honoring my enemies with my faith for them, and faith for those who love me that it would be an honor to have faith for them to enrich their lives, hearts, minds and souls with humility like small children, for the healing of their souls for the Glory of God and his honor, honor, honor, and honor forever. Amen

Healing the nations

-Love Christ Jesus over 2,000 years ago.
    -Love Rainbow

If this book has blessed your soul, life, heart, and mind and you got healing from the lord. tell other people about this book, and practice these prayers between only you and the lord. the lord will bless your ministries, heal people's bodies in your ministries, and heal souls, and heal lives, and provide healing that needs to be done where pride and arrogance was. bless you greatly people, and i bless the nations and a people who don't mind prayer from someone who lives the childlike faith, and apply its wisdoms. I have blessed the nation's God's people, and ministered to the ones who salted my name. I've prayed for them in this book ive humbled myself like a child and to God the father be the glory and honor, and to christ jesus be the glory and all honor placed on their hearts. I have loved my lord's and I show my greatest honor for their hearts. for I have served my lords in childlike faith and his people must come out of pride and arrogance, or they could hear christ jesus say this ... .unless God's people humble themselves like a child they all will not go to heaven.-Matthew 18:3

Contact me at Rainbow.michelle55@aol.com if you want me to speak in your churches or events, if this book has blessed you and you want healing in your ministries and Godly love of christ jesus to break some things off your churches, reach me at that email.

Afterword

God Jesus my prize my bridegroom and God the father I'm your SUN

God Jesus this book of promises I have kept to you is my Divine offering to you and God the father to please you and give you the all the Glory and Honor, as promised when I was in front of my house, and to heal your heart lord Jesus and God the father, the healing of your heart lord Jesus and God the father is a promise kept by me thine angel, thine SUN, because of what your heart thinks about souls in these end times. May all the nations be healed from this healing book of pocket childlike faith prayers and give their lives to you. Divine Creative prayers to keep people's sins forgiven lord sin undone in your name. Living beyond the perfect will of Christ Jesus is a daily sacrifice of love and a healing mind because of what the enemy meant for evil. This book is an offering I make to the lord god the father, and christ jesus

About the Author

Rainbow is the author of this book prayers that rout out pride and arrogance healing the nations and she lives in St. louis Missouri with her mom and mom's daycare where Christ Jesus cultivated rainbow in the childlike faith and taught her humility and suffering for his sake, the joys and the gifts of humility has been her gift, and Christ Jesus dismantled pride in rainbows heart and mind, and she hath applied these teachings that Christ Jesus taught her, may people be blessed with humility if they find any joy in ministry other than making money of hurting people in their congregations, we do not want leave people the same in congregations we want to change their lives and not what pastors and bishops want from them their congregations. Their congregations should not be their only source of income. Leaderships, and believers must stop depending on their congregations for income and start looking at their true condition. Leaderships must come out their congregations' pockets and give Christ Jesus heart and not just in front of people where they are making money because ministry is not about what people have in their pockets, it's what they have in their hearts. when will gods people stop trusting and giving their souls to liars?